Mind, World, God: Science and Spirit in the 21st Century

Tam Hunt

Mind, World, God: Science and Spirit in the 21ˢᵗ Century

ISBN: 9780578189161

Contents

Preface

This book is about integration, unity, oneness. It is an attempt to show how we can integrate our various selves – social, biological, spiritual, etc. – into a larger sense of self, our *true* self. We are generally fractured beings, largely unaware of who we really are, sometimes working against ourselves. We can, with knowledge and practice, integrate our various selves and achieve internal harmony, which will of course lead to greater external harmony.

Integration is always beneficial. We don't have to be personally suffering or believe that life is necessarily suffering to desire greater integration. We simply have to believe that our lot could be improved significantly – a truth that I would hope all thinking persons will agree with. Suffering is very much a part of life, but its sting may be diminished in so many ways through knowledge and compassion, which result from better integration. Suffering based on ignorance need not define our lives, as it has for so much of human history, indeed, as it has defined so much of our eons-long biological history that extends far beyond our human history. While Nature may often be "red in tooth and claw," she is more generally compassionate and gentle when we truly know her.

Ultimately, this book is about love. Yes, it's a love story! All things, when we understand them deeply, reduce to oneness and that oneness is love. Continuing the long history of various traditions both East and West, this book attempts to show how we are, each of us, capable of unconditional love, but also worthy of receiving unconditional love. This human and divine love extends not only to every human being, but to all creatures, and onward to every stone, molecule, and atom of the universe. *It's all one thing, pure love, and we are it.*

The aim of philosophy is to see the world as a unity; to understand it in terms of a single, all-encompassing principle.

20th Century American philosopher and religious scholar

Huston Smith

Part I: A fine balance

"Spiritual but not religious" has become cliché because it's true. We are in the early 21st Century increasingly rejecting organized religion in favor of a more authentic and individualized spirituality. The fastest-growing religious movement seems to be that of no religion.

There are many reasons for this transformation, including the growth of alternative explanations about the "big questions" about the nature of life, consciousness, meaning, purpose, which are in many cases increasingly being provided by modern science. Many of us are also rejecting the overly restrictive or outdated moral rules that many traditional religions impose. Reading the Old Testament book Leviticus today, for example, with its sentences of death for adultery or homosexuality, or prohibitions against wearing clothing of wool and linen together, is a surreal experience. "We're supposed to believe this?" many of us ask ourselves. Similarly outdated rules exist in most of today's religions.

Modern science has problems of its own in terms of providing meaning and purpose. Science has in many cases gone too far in attempting to eradicate meaning, intention, and consciousness, from our explanations and from our universe. If we take mainstream physics, chemistry and biology on face value, it provides a rather depressing picture of humanity and our role in the universe.

What ideas should fill the gap in our psyches, if we are turned off, as many of us are, by traditional religion and find mainstream science too austere? How do we honor our need to find meaning and purpose in our lives, if we are suspicious of the answers offered by traditional religion, and also want to apply reason and science as much as faith in developing our own spiritual views?

This book is an extended answer to these questions.

I am fortunate to have enjoyed a profoundly mystical experience in my early twenties. This experience seared itself into my heart and mind one night as I lay on my brother's couch in Seattle. I had spent the evening out at a coffee shop and a bar with my brother and my father, talking with each other and with friends. We ended the evening out by returning to my brother's apartment, where we were staying. After chatting a bit more we all went to bed, me to the couch in the living room.

Upon closing my eyes to sleep I quickly found myself overcome by psychic waves of joy and comfort, each one more powerful than the last. Lying on the couch, with eyes closed, I felt engulfed by love. I saw a bright white light and felt myself drawn to it. Pure ecstasy is the closest description I can give. This kind of white light vision seems to have been experienced by many others throughout human history. Upon seeing and feeling the white light, I felt a deep oneness with all of nature, my fellow human beings, and a dissolution of the ego. *Seeing God* is as good a description of this experience as any – and many who have enjoyed experiences like mine describe it this way.

Here's the catch: I was high on marijuana when the vision occurred to me. For many years I discounted this experience as drug-induced and thus "merely" an interesting psychological phenomenon that had happened to me. I was at that time an opinionated atheist, after having been raised an agnostic and after having spent some time in my childhood in a 60s-style commune where "God talk" was common. I had developed a healthy skepticism toward religion and spirituality, due in part to the break-up of the commune, which occurred after revelations about the sexual and financial improprieties of its founder, combined with my growing knowledge about traditional religion and its many downsides.

I was, from a fairly young age drawn to Eastern mysticism and read voraciously through some of the Buddhist and Taoist writers, at the same time that I read many Western philosophers, including Bertrand Russell, a well-known British 20th Century atheist who was also active in the anti-war movements of his era.

I was attracted to Buddhism because it seemed to make sense to me and it didn't require belief in a deity. Buddhism is more of a psychology and philosophy of life than a religion (but yes, it is still a religion). It's mostly a way of managing emotions and negative thinking, and ultimately a way to find lasting peace. Buddhism doesn't necessarily exclude God, in most of its many, sometimes conflicting, variations. But it generally doesn't highlight the role of any kind of personal God and the historical Buddha apparently chose to stay quiet on this topic in his direct teachings.

I found many aspects of the Buddhist approach to the big questions appealing and it allowed me to develop my spiritual views further while at the same time I continued to reject the concept of God in my life or in the universe more generally.

Things change, and I continued to think, read, discuss, and experience. I have now, based on the initial impetus of my early mystical experience and my ongoing purely intellectual investigations, arrived at a place where I can say that I accept a role for (what we may as well call) God in the universe and in my set of concepts that help me understand the universe. But the God I'm referring to is not a personal God either. I've transformed over time from being an agnostic to an atheist to an untraditional theist.

My many years of thinking about the nature of mind or consciousness was key to this transformation. I view mind, defined simply as subjectivity, a center of awareness, as ubiquitous in nature. As matter complexifies, so mind complexifies. Mind is a continuum from simplicity to complexity that develops as the universe is populated by increasingly complex collections of matter. The collections arise through physical and biological evolutionary processes.

There is a tendency in some of today's spiritual traditions to refer to "mind" as that which distracts us from our true self. I am not using this term in this sense. Again, mind is in this book simply a generic term for subjectivity, consciousness, experience, or simply having a perspective, a center of perception.

Even though my version of God is by no means a traditional notion of a personal God (a God that relates to us directly as individuals), it is God nonetheless. I feel confident in the notion of God as Source, the ocean of being from which all of reality emanates. God as Summit, a conscious entity, regardless of whether it has any role in our lives, is not as clear to me. I haven't personally felt a conscious God speaking to me, but I can't rule it out as a possibility. I do find it unlikely, nevertheless, that any higher intelligence worthy of the name God would take an active role in our lives, as many traditions claim.

Source, however – *Brahman,* the ocean or ground of being, or whatever name you prefer – has been established in my life as a very real entity, through experience, insight and meditation. Through contemplation and meditation, it seems, we can remind ourselves of our identity with Source. It is through both my own experiences and the many lines of reasoning discussed in this book that I know the ocean of being, God as Source, is real and that it is the source from which we all spring, from which all things spring, including God as Summit. This is the case whether God as Summit exists now or, perhaps, is coming into existence in the future as we co-create this entity. But Source is itself always changing, underlining the one constant of our universe: change, at every level of reality. Nothing exists outside of time, even Source.

I do my best (not always succeeding) to re-establish this mystical connection between my embodied self and Source on an on-going basis, intellectually and viscerally, in my heart and bones. It is through this connection to God as Source that I find a perpetual and infinite source of happiness, meaning, and wholeness. The hard part in living this human life is to keep this insight in mind and not get too distracted by more fleeting sources of happiness.

This is my own path and it is certainly not for everyone. I don't call myself a Buddhist and there are some aspects of Buddhism that I don't find convincing, or at least that I view with suspicion (karma and reincarnation, for example). Many schools of Buddhism reject the notion of a ground/ocean of being or Brahman, which is a concept that I find fundamental and compelling. I'm very attracted to Vedanta Hinduism (which is based on knowing Brahman and our identity with Brahman) and Taoism, but I don't label myself as part of these traditions either. Rather, I generally reject labels, and this is my broader point: many people are now choosing to reject all religious labels. We are, instead, choosing our own paths, guided by intuition and reason as much or more than by tradition and authority.

Yogananda, an Indian mystic in the Kriya Yoga tradition, said it well: "Everything else can wait, but your search for God cannot wait." In our search for authentic spirituality, experience seems to precede reason for most people. Words and concepts only go so far. For others, experience without a rational basis for spiritual views is not enough. For yet others, reason alone may well be enough to accept God/Source as real, even without the profound direct experience of God as Source or as Summit.

We're all different, and this is, perhaps the most important insight we can take from the trend away from organized religion toward a more authentic spirituality. Buddha reportedly said in his last teachings: "Be a light unto yourself." Don't take anything on faith or on authority. Explore, challenge, read, think, discuss. Experience.

Part I of this book summarizes the key themes and ideas fleshed out in the rest of the book. Part II presents some thoughts on thinking – an overview of the tools we have to construct a spirituality based on both reason and faith. Parts III through VII then use these tools to do just that, describing an approach to understanding the universe and our place in it that draws on many great minds and hearts, including Alfred North Whitehead, Pierre Teilhard de Chardin, Alan Watts, Arthur Schopenhauer, modern physics and biology, the Upanishads, Buddha, Christ, and the great mystics of many spiritual traditions.

[A beneficial post-modern] science ... will try to live up to its name, which simply means knowledge, and will not therefore arbitrarily exclude some kinds of knowledge as inherently "unscientific." ... With such a science, not only the modern warfare but even the modern boundary between science and theology will, in principle at least, be overcome. ... The distinction will be one of degree, not kind.

20th Century American philosopher and religious scholar David Ray Griffin

Religion and science are the two conjugated faces or phases of one and the same complete act of knowledge – the only one which can embrace the past and future of evolution so as to contemplate, measure and fulfill them.

20th Century French anthropologist and theologian Pierre Teilhard de Chardin (1959)

Chapter 1: Faith and reason are compatible

Science and spirituality are often discussed as though they are fundamentally different endeavors. When we drill down deeply, however, we see that they're actually different faces of the same endeavor. Science and spirituality are both about understanding, integration, unification. This book attempts to show how we can achieve a deep integration of our various selves. It also attempts to show that the scientific and spiritual impulses – and even methods – are in fact part of the same grand endeavor to understand and appreciate the marvels of our universe. Science emphasizes reason, but every good scientist will acknowledge that faith is very much part of what she does – even if it is only faith in the ability of science to deliver useful answers.

Spiritual traditions often emphasize faith over reason, but every good spiritual leader will encourage seekers to pursue an empirical path to individual spirituality – that is, a path that seeks inner and outer *testing* of the various insights offered.

"Faith" is often used to suggest acceptance of statements that seem to contradict reason. "Faith" in this meaning is the same as "blind faith." Faith has another meaning, however, which refers to making a choice between whatever alternatives are possible when faced with a lack of definitive evidence. By exercising faith we make a decision that is not otherwise supported by good evidence. This is quite different from the first meaning. Rather than accepting statements blindly even when they contradict reason or one's intuitions – the first meaning – the second meaning refers to making a choice, hopefully well-reasoned, among plausible alternatives despite a lack of good evidence. In this way it is clear that faith and reason are not necessarily in conflict.

But these issues go much deeper, of course.

There is yet another meaning to "faith" that refers to spiritual or religious views in a general sense. A "person of faith" is a person who believes in God, Yahweh, Christ, Krishna, Muhammad or any religious tradition. A person of faith is someone who prioritizes a religious view of the world over non-religious views. In this way there would seem to be a deep conflict between faith and reason. We shall see, however, that this is not necessarily the case. We can be deeply spiritual and rational at the same time.

Jesus got a lot of things right, so did Buddha, and so did Muhammad, the Hindu rishis and Jewish mystics. In fact, just about every spiritual tradition, when we get down to their essentials, taps into many of the same underlying original insights. Times, places and cultures differ and for these reasons the emphasis and style of each tradition is of course different from every other tradition. But difference is to be expected. What is less expected is similarity. I label these similarities, which I will explore in this book, the "universal spiritual teachings" or the "perennial philosophy."

Science also gets a lot of things right, despite many mistakes and mis-steps along the way. Science often distinguishes itself from spirituality in that science emphasizes, by its very nature, the scientific/experimental method. In the scientific method, hypotheses are posed based on initial observations, more specific data is gathered and compared to the initial hypotheses. If hypotheses are supported by the data, they become "theories." If data contradict a particular hypothesis, it is modified or scrapped entirely. Through this constant give and take between intuition, induction, data gathering and deduction, science allows us to grope through the dark vastness of the universe and create an intelligent abstract *model* of that dark universe. As we shall see later, we can never *know* the universe in terms of its fundamental reality. All we can do is create models and test those models. If the models withstand many tests, we consider the model provisionally accurate – until an experiment produces data to contradict the model.

Models and theories are never proven, only supported. As Gregory Bateson, the 20th Century British biologist and philosopher, put it: "Science probes, it does not prove." Nothing is ever proven in science; it is only supported or falsified (contradicted). If data falsify a model or theory, we modify the theory or start anew in our model-making.

This is the scientific method in a very small nutshell.

When we compare these two fundamental human endeavors, science and religion, we see that reason and faith are complementary, not contradictory, in both of these grand endeavors. Faith should not be blind. It should instead be a rational response to a lack of evidence in any specific inquiry. Reason should not be dogmatic. It should instead be humble and honest. Where reason and evidence cannot speak, there faith may step in.

Despite the overly strident denials of religion by the "new atheists" in the early part of the 21st Century, there is much that science will never be able to tell us, and much that spirituality can provide. This is the case because a basic problem we face as intelligent creatures, trying to make sense of it all, is that we can't know with certainty whether the universe is in fact a rational place. Does the universe always operate based on predictable and discoverable rules? Do these rules – often described as "laws" of physics, chemistry, etc. – apply equally in all places? Do they change over time? The bottom line is that we can't ever know the answers to these questions. All we truly *know*, as Descartes and many other philosophers have pointed out, is that the perceiver exists: "I think, therefore I am." *Everything else is conjecture and supposition, more or less supported by evidence but never known with certainty.*

This is a highly important point that bears repeating: all each of us knows with any certainty is the reality of our own experience; everything else beyond our direct experience is conjecture and supposition.

We are indeed groping in the dark in trying to impose a rational framework on the stuff of the universe.

We are, however, offered strong intimations of a rational universe based simply on the undeniable fact that the impressive scientific edifice built over the course of a few thousand years has produced so many technological miracles. We've certainly figured many things out, demonstrating the usefulness of the scientific method. Who could have imagined three hundred years ago, in Newton's time, that we would enjoy the marvels of smartphones, the Internet, flat screen TVs, space flight, bionic limbs and other marvels of modern medicine, and have been able to plumb the depths and the heights of the cosmos as we have? It is truly incredible. Yet...

We shall never know if the universe is always predictable in its rules, in all times and in all places, as many think it is. It's ultimately a matter of faith if we believe that the universe is a rational place. This conjecture, that the universe is rational, can't be proven because we can never know the full extent of what we don't know and, as mentioned, science does not *prove* anything.

These difficulties in establishing the validity of a rational universe will perhaps be welcome news for many who prefer to prioritize spirituality over science. Unfortunately, this prioritization is common today because for many hundreds of years there has been overt conflict between science and spirituality. These two aspects of the human experience, science and spirit, are often presented as compartmentalized activities. One part of our brain, so it seems, is the "science module" and another part the "religion module." This is the case in our society more generally, with too few people capable of sober and respectful discussion of both broad fields. But there is no *necessary* contradiction or incompatibility between science and religion. It is undeniable, of course, that there are many contradictions between *specific* religious or spiritual doctrines and scientific doctrines. For example, did God literally create the world in seven days, as described in Genesis, the first book of the Hebrew and Christian Bibles? No. This is, at best, a poetic metaphor for creation. The broader point is that the spiritual and scientific impulses, which exist to some degree within each of us, are ultimately the *same impulse.* They are manifestations of the yearning for understanding, for belonging, and for integration.

The way to truly reconcile science and religion is to craft a rational spirituality, what Ken Wilber, the contemporary American philosopher and cultural critic, calls "deep science." A *rational* spirituality is possible and has been presented by many spiritual traditions in some form for millennia, and explored further by many modern authors and thinkers. In a rational spirituality, we don't need to take spiritual insight "on faith." We can rationally examine and explore offered insights and arrive at our own synthesis. Some faith is necessary for mere existence – all we *know* with any certainty is the reality of our own subjective experience in each moment.

We must take some shuffling steps forward based on faith, hands outstretched into the dark, to proceed beyond this most basic truth. Reason and faith are unavoidable aspects of human existence, the yin and yang of life, the male and female aspects of the upwelling of consciousness from its primordial beginnings into its present human form that we each know and enjoy.

The only thing you need to know to
understand the deepest metaphysical secrets
is this: that for every outside there is an
inside and for every inside there is
an outside, and although they are different,
they go together.

20th Century British philosopher and scholar
of religions Alan Watts, *The Myth of Myself*

Through my scientific work I have come to
believe more and more strongly that the
universe is put together with an ingenuity so
astonishing that I cannot accept it merely as
brute fact. ... I have come to the point of view
that mind – i.e., conscious awareness of the
world – is not a meaningless and incidental
quirk of nature, but an absolutely fundamental
facet of reality.

American physicist Paul Davies, *The Mind of*
God: The Scientific Basis for a Rational World

Chapter 2: Consciousness is the bridge between science and spirit

We cannot separate our thinking about science and religion from thinking itself – what is generally labeled "consciousness." Consciousness is a crucial link in this broader examination of science and religion. But what is consciousness? Who am "I"? What is the awareness that seems to be situated somewhere behind my eyes and between my ears? These questions are part of the classic mind/body problem that has delighted and stumped philosophers for eons. There are many answers to these questions and it is up to each of us to decide, based on our intuitions and personal brand of reason, which are the most appropriate or helpful answers. I offer here some answers that I think provide particular insight into the nature of reality more generally – and provide that key link between science and spirituality.

Human consciousness is a type of experience. Experience is *what it is like to be something.* What is it like to be you (instead of me)? What is it like to be a dog, a mouse, a bacterium, a bat? What is it like to be an electron, a star, a galaxy, the universe? Maybe there is not something it is like to be a bacterium, an electron, or a galaxy. Or maybe there is.

The consciousness that humans enjoy, often called "self-consciousness," is a complex type of experience that involves, crucially, a model of itself in the larger model of the universe that is contained within our head. As we grow, from birth through adulthood and beyond, each of us develops an increasingly complex model of the universe. It starts fairly simple; though certainly not as a blank slate (it is clear that many skills and basic understandings are built into our little brains as they are formed in the womb, as part of the many billions of years of evolutionary heritage we enjoy merely by successfully navigating our way out of the womb). The model each of us creates grows in complexity and, generally around the age of one or two years, it becomes complex enough that it includes a "self" in that model. What was initially a model of basic sensory experience – the raw data of our senses – is complexified to the point where the hands, legs, torso and the tip of a nose each of us see and feel, and the references by our parents and others we interact with to "you," your name, or various terms of endearment, are combined into a concept of the self. This concept of the self is integral to the human experience, though it is a double-edged sword. More on this in later chapters...

It is initially difficult for us, as creatures who enjoy the benefits of a complex sense of self, to project our awareness into a place less complex, a place that doesn't enjoy a self. But we can do this if we temporarily reduce *experience* to its constituents. Experience, of any type, requires just three features: a subject (the center of experience), an object, and a link between the two. The link is causal and physical, by definition. Joseph Campbell mirrors this point in his book, *Myths of Light: Eastern Metaphors of the Eternal*: "For there to be an object, there must be a subject of knowledge and a relationship between them." For example, a newborn baby is a subject – it experiences. The baby perceives a ball, an object. The ball is perceived through its influence on the universe around it, the various forces it emits or reflects, which include visible light (electromagnetism), its weight (gravity), and other physical properties the ball enjoys. Perception of the ball in this case includes the baby chewing on it. Again: at its most basic level, experience involves a subject, an object and a link between the two. We generally call the link "perception."

Most of us have no trouble grasping the essence of "object" or "link." But thinking about what types of things are "subjects" can often present great difficulties. With our human experience as a subject, we are inclined to accord subject status, an inside, only to things sufficiently like us – other primates, furry mammals, and perhaps some other less complex creatures. But we realize when we think through the nature of experience that some kind of experience very likely goes all the way down to the simplest things, including bats, rats, bacteria and even non-living processes like electrons. The basic reasoning here is simple: when we look at the biological world we don't see large jumps in form or function; rather, we see generally incremental steps and incremental changes over times. If the external forms of our biological world reflect incremental differences and incremental changes isn't it most likely that consciousness reflects similar incremental differences and changes?

As Alan Watts, the 20th Century British philosopher and religious scholar, explained in his inimitable style (imagine a beautiful educated British accent): "For every outside there is an inside and for every inside there is an outside." Why? It's all about the third component of experience, the "link," which provides insight back upon what it is to be a subject.

I have conceptually de-constructed experience into three features, the subject, object and link between the two. But we must keep in mind that this deconstruction is purely conceptual because no such deconstruction is possible in reality due to the fact that experience is an ongoing and necessarily holistic process. Nevertheless, the conceptual deconstruction is helpful in many ways. The link, which we call perception in creatures like ourselves, is at its most basic level simply *reception*. In other words, the link between every subject and every object can take many forms but at its most basic it is simply reception of some influence from an object by the subject. This reception doesn't require biological sensory structures like eyes, tongues or ears. Indeed, an electron in the depths of space receives information from the universe around it in the form of very weak gravitational and electromagnetic influences. To "be in the universe" means there is some link between the item at issue and the rest of the universe. If there was no such link, the item at issue would *not be in the universe* because it would have absolutely no interaction with the universe. Thus, an electron in the depths of space is in the universe (it exists) by virtue of its reception of even the most faint forces around it. It *receives* this information. The electron may be considered, then, a subject; the source of the influence felt by the electron is an object; and the link between the two is the reception of information. We see now that the three key ingredients of experience seem to be present even for a lonely electron: subject, object and link. So, again, perception is in a more general sense simply reception of some causal influence by a subject. This process is literally universal and does not require any biological sensory organs.

Does this reception/perception process have to include a subject? We can't say with certainty that this is the case because the only experience we know with certainty is our own. But we can say, by breaking our own experience down to its most basic level – subject, object, link – that this same process is present in all material things, literally. This is highly suggestive that even for the lonely electron, for example, the notions of experience and subjectivity are relevant, even if only in some extremely rudimentary way. If this is the case, experience goes all the way down, though it becomes highly attenuated the further down we go. The experience in a subatomic particle like an electron is most likely nothing more than a basic humming of sheer existence and movement and thus very little like our human existence or even like the experience of an amoeba.

I have thus far described the "link" between subject and object as perception or more generally as *reception*. However, the whole three-part process is in fact perception/reception because there is no such thing as perception without a subject and an object. There is no disembodied or unmoored perception. More generally, we see that consciousness itself is completely synonymous with perception/reception. There is always consciousness *of*, experience *of*. There is no consciousness without a subject, an object, and a link between the two. ("Consciousness without an object" is, however, one description of certain kinds of mystical experience, an issue I delve into in later chapters).

We have in this discussion strayed far from human experience and this may seem too abstract a discussion to be very relevant or useful. It is, however, one of the key insights linking science to spirituality. If we realize that every inside has an outside and every outside has an inside – that is, all things *experience* to some degree – we realize that this process very likely goes up as well as down the great chain of being. If the electron, the rat, the bat, the cat, the dog and the human all experience, why can't there be higher levels of experience? Why can't a complex experience exist within a star, a galaxy, the universe? There would seem to be no basic principle preventing such an experience from existing. After all, there is an experience right here, here behind my eyes and between my ears, which no other experiencer can *know*. Only I can know *this* experiencer from the inside. Even though I can't know with any certainty the nature of other experiencers, I do know with certainty that there is at least one experiencer, me, and I can through many lines of reasoning deduce the existence of experience in many other things, including other humans, bats, rats, cats, electrons and perhaps stars, galaxies or the universe as a whole.

The reader needn't accept these arguments on face value at this point. This is an introduction. The rest of the book explains these concepts further and presents many other lines of evidence to support it. The view that some type of consciousness goes all the way down the chain of being is known as *panpsychism* or *panexperientialism*. This set of ideas has been developed by many thinkers over the last few thousand years, including the sages of India during the second and first millennia BCE, Heraclitus and other pre-Socratic philosophers in ancient Greece, Plato and Aristotle, Plotinus in the 3rd Century CE, Spinoza and Leibniz in the 17th Century, Schopenhauer and Fichte in the 19th Century in Germany, William James, Henri Bergson, Alfred North Whitehead, Pierre Teilhard de Chardin, Charles Hartshorne, John Cobb, Jr., Freeman Dyson, David Ray Griffin, David Bohm, Galen Strawson, Ken Wilber and many others in the 20th Century, and an increasing number of prominent thinkers in the 21st Century. Panpsychism is catching on as a viable solution to the long-standing "mind/body problem" *and* also provides the key bridge between science and spirituality.

Further support for this expansive view of consciousness may be found in the degree to which it is helpful as a hypothesis in many different fields. The idea that all things have some degree of experience cuts through Gordian Knots in physics, biology, and spirituality, like a hot knife through butter. Some of these knots are discussed in later chapters. This is suggestive that panpsychism may in fact be an accurate view about the nature of the universe and not just a philosopher's flight of imagination.

Some biologists and philosophers have described the idea of evolution by natural selection, what is known today as neo-Darwinism, as a "universal acid" because of its immensely potent explanatory power. I agree that the principle of evolution is indeed a universal acid and later chapters flesh out this view (with some qualifications). The idea that all things are experiential – panpsychism – is an explanatory theme on a par with the principle of evolution. Indeed, it multiplies the explanatory power of the principle of evolution because it builds upon that power. Panpsychism can be thought of as a "transcendental acid" because it helps explain not only difficult problems in biology, but also in physics, philosophy, spirituality and practically every other area of human inquiry.

A consciousness without an object is no consciousness.

19th Century German philosopher Arthur Schopenhauer.

Apart from the experience of subjects there is nothing, nothing, nothing, bare nothingness

20th Century philosopher, mathematician and physicist Alfred North Whitehead, *Process and Reality* (1929)

Chapter 3: Materialism threw out the baby with the bathwater

The recent resurgence of panpsychism has sprung from the failure of today's conventional materialist worldview, the *scientistic* and dogmatic belief that all things, including consciousness, can be explained through the non-experiential matter, space and time of our prevailing theories of physics. The basic worldview of today's materialism is as follows:

- "Matter" or "matter/energy" (considered two sides of the same coin) is the primary stuff of the universe

- Each type of matter or matter/energy consists of persistent objects called particles, which are all identical within each type

- The vast majority of matter is non-experiential, non-conscious, non-subjective, including the fundamental units of matter and most collections of fundamental units

- It's only when a certain level of biological complexity is reached that rudimentary consciousness arises

- The framework of physics is "causally closed," which means that physics can at least in principle explain everything worth explaining and all things, even human interactions, are ultimately caused by the microphysical interactions at the level of atoms and subatomic particles

Richard Dawkins, a British biologist, and Daniel Dennett, an American philosopher, may be considered two of the key standard-bearers for materialism in the early part of the 21st Century. These authors have contributed much to our world in terms of scientific and philosophical explanations. But they and their colleagues have overshot the mark. Inspired by the many successes of modern science and philosophy, they have become drunk on a certain brand of reason and, to use Yann Martel's phrase from his wonderful novel, *Life of Pi*, missed the "better story" about the nature of the universe.

Materialism has reigned largely unchallenged in mainstream scientific and philosophical circles for over a century now. Its prominence was cemented with the publication of Charles Darwin's immensely influential *Origin of Species*, his first significant work setting down his ideas on natural selection and the transformation of species over time through processes that don't require any intelligent design. Like many intellectual movements, however, the powerful insights of Darwin's theories led many to throw the proverbial baby out with the bathwater. What is known as "neo-Darwinism" (described more in later chapters) today is far more fundamentalist and dogmatic than Darwin was himself. We face now, with today's hyper-materialism, the threat of a new dogmatism that may perhaps be as damaging to human development and self-realization as the dogmatism of medieval religious traditions.

A key result of Darwin's theory in the 19th and 20th Centuries was a rejection by many intellectuals of the "argument from design" for the existence of God. The basic argument is quite simple: the natural world, with all its many wondrous creatures, is far too complex to be the result of purely random forces; ergo, there must be a designer and we may as well call that God. There are many good reasons to doubt this argument and, indeed, the argument from design is rejected by just about every scientist and philosopher in the modern era. But the ejection of God and discussions of Nature's divinity more generally from mainstream scientific discourse, based on the rejection of the argument from design, goes too far. It substitutes one dogma for another: dogmatic materialism instead of dogmatic theism.

This ejection of God from serious discussion by scientists and philosophers was aided by the tremendous successes of modern physics, medicine and psychology in the 19th and 20th Centuries. Despite the ongoing debate with respect to the role of consciousness in quantum mechanics, many philosophers and scientists, and an increasing number of the populace at large, began to imagine a universe consisting of nothing but glorified billiard balls – tiny billiard balls we call particles. In this view, it's all just little particles (or wave/particles, as some versions of quantum theory assert) bouncing off each other under well-established rules that we call physics. The conventional materialist worldview asserts that somehow, at some apparently arbitrary mid-point in the grand chain of being, consciousness, the inside of matter, springs into being. Where before there was only the outside of matter, suddenly an inside sprang into being. Where there was only a universe of objects, the first subject springs into being. In other words, "a miracle occurs..."

Panpsychism asserts that it is more sensible to suppose that the inside of matter was there from the very beginning, albeit in highly rudimentary form. Far better for a miracle, if there must be a miracle that produces consciousness, to occur at the beginning of the chain of being than at some apparently arbitrary mid-point. As matter complexified so experience and consciousness complexified, in an ongoing organic and continuous process. We are its highest expression in this corner of the universe. We are special, but not in the way our natural chauvinism suggests. We are special due to the highly concentrated and complex form of experience we enjoy. But this is not a difference in kind – we are organically part of the universe and enjoy the same benefits of sheer being as all other parts of our universe. What we enjoy as experience is a difference in *degree*. And that difference in degree is very unlikely to stop at our level of existence, the human level. There are likely higher levels above the "merely" human, not in different dimensions as is suggested in various spiritual traditions, but rather in different forms and different scales of space and time.

This is a key link between science and spirit: the realization that all matter has some degree of experience and that the process that leads to complex experience in us, as human beings, likely leads to higher levels of experience far beyond human comprehension.

I do not make any clear distinction between mind and God. God is what mind becomes when it has passed beyond the scale of our comprehension.

20th Century American physicist Freeman Dyson , *Infinite In All Directions* (1988)

Chapter 4: You are the universe, we are the universe

We have been discussing "the universe" as though we know what it is. But what is it, really? Under the generally accepted definition, the universe is everything. It's all there is, period. Words mean what we want them to mean, however, as young Humpty Dumpty reminds us: "When I use a word, it means what I choose it to mean, neither more nor less." In this book, I use "universe" to mean the sum of our perceptible, physical reality. The universe is the sum total of the objects available to our senses, which we assume to be "out there," as opposed to "in here," in our heads. This is not a real distinction, however, because everything inside our heads is also part of the universe. We can never, however, *know* the true nature of those objects, the "thing in itself," to use the celebrated German philosopher Immanuel Kant's phrase. This is an insight that goes back at least to Plato, who described our limitations in his cave allegory, as follows.

Plato asks us to imagine a person who is forced to live in a cave all of his life, completely bound, to the point where his eyes are forced to look ahead at all times. This unfortunate person must watch the back of the cave, on which shadows flicker from a fire's bright light behind the prisoner. The captors perform their routine activities behind the prisoner and their shadows are cast on the wall.

The prisoner, knowing no other reality, mistakes the shadows for reality, not realizing they are cast by the captors behind him.

This is how our life really is. We are prisoners bound by our perceptions and fooled into thinking our perceptions reflect the ultimate reality. It is not that our perceived reality is unreal or illusory. No, it is real, but it is not as real or as accurate as we think it is. There are levels and there are levels.

All we generally know are our perceptions, our experience, what Kant called the world of phenomena. To be sure, we can deduce certain insights about the nature of reality that aren't directly dependent on perception, as Kant pointed out, but even these deductions are based ultimately on perception from our eons-long biological heritage. Some traditions and modern thinkers also suggest that we can perceive with additional senses, the eye of the mind, but we needn't visit that issue at this time.

Despite the limitations of our senses and the recognition that the world we think is real perceptible reality is instead a creation of our brains, minds and senses, we can compare our perceptions with other people and gain a pretty good idea of what comprises our shared universe beyond our imperfect perceptions. This shared perceptible reality is what I call the universe.

Are we, as subjective entities, part of the universe? Clearly we are. We exist "in the universe" because we can perceive the objects in our universe. If we couldn't perceive the universe, we wouldn't be in it, part of it. We are part of the universe due to the same process of reception/perception discussed previously. We are the subject, the universe is the sum total of all perceivable objects, and the links connecting us to those objects consist of the various forces by which information is transmitted between subjects and objects, including gravity and electromagnetism (visible light, ultraviolet, radio waves, etc.). We are, in turn, an object for all other subjects in the universe. What is a subject for one is an object for another, and vice versa: all insides have an outside and all outsides have an inside.

Each of us is in the universe, part of the universe. But where are the boundaries for each self, each subject? Where do I end and you begin? Where do I end and all other objects in the universe begin? There is clearly some kind of split between myself and the rest of the universe, otherwise I wouldn't have the feeling of "myself." An obvious and tempting answer is that "I" consist of my body and where it ends I end. But what if I lose a leg, is that leg still part of me? Most of us would quickly answer "no." What if I lost all my limbs? Most of us would also answer that my limbs are now not part of me. I am, however, still here and consist, it seems, of what remains of my body.

What if I "lost" my entire body, through an advanced surgical procedure that is not yet possible, and was reduced to a brain in a vat? Is the brain "me" or is my still-functioning body "me"? Imagine I am allowed to look at my own brain in a vat separate from my body. Imagine I am touching my own brain and pondering why it still feels like "I" am in my head somewhere behind my eyes even though my brain is right there in my hands.

Such strange and unlikely scenarios are surely improbable, but they are not at all impossible. And because they are not impossible they warrant serious discussion of their impacts on our sense of self and identity. So where does my *self* reside?

Let's consider the possibility that "I" am in my brain, separate from my body. What about when I fall asleep, am "I" still there when I dream? Am "I" still there during the deepest non-dreaming sleep? We can track brain activity using various tools and we can see the parts of the brain that are active at different times. Activity is always changing, with different configurations leading to a slightly different sense of self in each different moment. It's still quite a mystery today as to how exactly the brain and body work their magic in producing an "I." What is clear, however, is that our sense of self cannot be localized to any particular part of the brain or even any particular type of pattern in the brain.

We can easily envision additional scenarios, less realistic because they require new technologies, in which the boundaries and permanence of the physical self are even less clear. What if my brain, the presumably key center of my cognitive self, was gradually replaced by computer chips emulating each neuron exactly? If my entire brain is replaced with computer chips, emulating the entire functioning of my brain exactly, am "I" still there? What if the exact same structure of my brain is copied onto a robot or a disembodied silicon brain? What if the "wet" biological structure of my normal brain was reproduced in a future teleportation machine and my present body destroyed as part of that teleportation process? These thought experiments, while not possible with today's technologies but conceivably possible with tomorrow's technologies, should show that establishing where I begin and the universe ends is not as clear as it seems upon first examination. In other words, establishing where "I" reside is highly problematic. All answers seem to fail. So where am "I"?

Taking a different approach, we can see that the universe is in actuality one unbroken whole due to the same subject, object, link trio introduced earlier. To be in the universe, everything in the universe must have a link to some other part of the universe. It's all one vast interconnected web. *It's all just one grand process.* There is no clear boundary between any one thing and any other thing, particularly when we realize that change is omnipresent. We cannot define accurately what is always changing – a realization stated as early as Aristotle. The objects we identify around us, and ourselves in our own internal model of reality, are in permanent flux, linked in each moment to everything around us, directly or indirectly. We introduce conceptual boundaries as tools to understand the diversity we are inundated with. But these conceptual boundaries are just that: conceptual. The actual boundaries don't really exist in any rigid, ultimate manner. Boundaries are a matter of convenience. Equally, the conventional sense of self as my body or my brain is a matter of convenience. It works for almost all aspects of everyday life. But it's not true.

If all things are linked in one vast web in constant flux, ultimately there is just one thing, one process: the universe itself. If we cannot separate ourselves from the universe, we are part and parcel of that universe. This is a key point. *It's all one just one thing, and we are it.* We cannot establish where we end and the universe begins or where the universe ends and we begin. I am my body. I am my mind. I am the chair I sit upon. I am the room where I sit. I am the planet I rest upon. I am the solar system, the galaxy, the universe. I can look to the most far-flung nebula, in its coruscating glory, and say *that is me.* It's all me. And you. I am the universe, you are the universe, we are the universe.

I shall have more to say on these insights in later chapters and I will discuss how my particular approach to the philosophical problem of consciousness – the "hard problem" – allows us to both see how each individual consciousness is formed in each moment, but also how that insight allows us to see that our true self, our deeper self, is the totality and not the experience we have as human becomings in each moment.

*Are not the mountains, waves, and skies a part
Of me and of my soul, as I of them?*

Lord Byron, *Childe Harold's Pilgrimage*, III

*The universe is an emanation, in which the infinite
realm of possibilities within God are being unfolded.*

David Ray Griffin, *Primordial Truth and Postmodern
Theology*

Chapter 5: You are God, we are God

Nature's divinity, often known as God, is another victim of language. Divinity may be felt, intuited. Or it may be deduced, as suggested in Chapter 2, by thinking through the nature of consciousness. This is just one of many possible lines of deduction for establishing the appropriate attitude toward nature's divinity.

The fact that there is something rather than nothing – existence itself – is another even more compelling demonstration of divinity. *Actuality* is physical, perceptible reality, the universe. *Potentiality* is the ability to create actuality, to create a universe. In other words, to have actuality, we must have potentiality. Why is there something rather than nothing? Why is there an entire vast and mysterious universe rather than nothing nothing nothing? We shall never know the answer to this question. But the fact that there *is* something – an entire universe – is a key clue to the nature of that universe and how it arises. All actuality must, it seems, come from pure potentiality. Modern physics supports this idea in finding that particles are popping into and out of existence perpetually in each tiniest corner of the universe. What we think of as empty space is, rather, a seething mass of activity.

I like to call this potentiality the *ocean of being*, the ground of being, or Source. Choose your favorite metaphor. One of its more ancient names is *Brahman*, in the Hindu Upanishadic tradition, which extends back at least four thousand years. Modern physics calls it the *vacuum* or *pure potentiality*. But it's not really nothing, as the term "vacuum" wrongly suggests. It is, rather, everything, but in potential form rather than actual form. One Nobel Prize-winning physicist, Frank Wilczek, has revived the term "ether" to describe this potentiality. Each moment of actuality springs forth from the fertile ocean of being, of Source. Source is the ultimate brute fact. There is nothing more fundamental, nothing below Source.

If the universe is one vast unbroken web, all *one process*, is Source distinct from this vast oneness? No. It is part and parcel of this oneness. It is the larger unity that subsumes and produces the unity that is the physical universe. While we can conceptually distinguish actuality from potentiality, yet again this distinction must melt away in reality. There is a perpetual dialectic between actuality and potentiality, manifest in the ongoing *creative advance* that lays down the universe in each moment as it springs forth from Source. Ultimately, all we can really say about the entirety of reality is *Om*. Om. Om. The word Om in Sanskrit is in fact

the symbol for the Hindu religion: ॐ.

We could just leave it at this.

Yet there are many good reasons to go beyond this one word spirituality, epistemology and ontology of Om. Our rational selves enjoy the play of concepts and there is clearly some type of multiplicity that manifests from the underlying oneness, the infinity of objects that comprises our universe. How does this multiplicity relate to oneness? Om is a fine answer. We could stop right there. But more detailed answers can help us in appreciating the profundity of the Om ontology. And, practically speaking, this book would be rather short if all I said was "Om."

In examining multiplicity, we can never isolate one object, in one moment in time, and say "this is x, right here, right now." We can *conceptually* isolate such an object, even freeze it in time and space, in our minds. But in actuality, we can do no such thing. The universe will not cooperate with our pleading to "please just stay still for one second so that we can get a good look at you." All is flux. Even the ocean of being, Brahman, must change in each moment in order to produce our physical universe. Action, creation, requires change, so even if the eternal ocean of being generally stays constant in its structure (whatever that is; we shall probably never know) we know that it too must change in order to produce the changing physical universe that we dwell in.

Source is sometimes described as "God," and there is nothing "wrong" about this label, as we discussed earlier. I prefer, however, to think of "twin ultimates," Source *and* God, as conceptual distinctions. In this context, it is God as Summit rather than God as Source that I am discussing. Source is the deepest, most fundamental level of existence

– God as Source. God as Summit is the highest, the grandest combination of experience. Source is not conscious, it is pure being, pure potentiality, pure creativity. God as Summit is, in the system I'm sketching here, by definition conscious to some degree, though probably in a very different way than we humans enjoy consciousness, if it exists at all (yet). Our long-term human mission may be to co-create Summit, to usher it into existence. Source and Summit are the twin ultimates that form the enclosing envelope for reality, the "lowest" and the "highest," the alpha and the omega. We are very much part of both Source and Summit. But we are also the entirety. We are all of it.

A visual aid is appropriate here to keep track of the various terms I've introduced:

	Source	*God*
Synonyms	Brahman, pure potentiality, vacuum, ether, akasha, apeiron, ein sof, ocean of being, ground of being, Buddha-nature, Godhead	Omega Point, Summit

To summarize: We realize now that the universe is one vast unbroken web of actuality; we are that universe, each of us, individually and together; the universe springs from the potentiality of the ground or ocean of being; there is no real separation between potentiality and actuality; we are, then, also Source; we are all of it, we are Nature's actuality, potentiality and divinity. I am Source, you are Source, we are Source. I am God, you are God, we are God.

This is the central realization common to all mystical traditions. One example from the wonderful book by Philip Kapleau, *Three Pillars of Zen*, is a 20th Century personal account from an American Buddhist who practiced for years in a Japanese Zen monastery. This account was written immediately after attaining *satori*:

> *Am totally at peace at peace at peace.*
> *Feel numb throughout body, yet hands and*
> *feet jumped for joy for almost half an hour.*
> *Am supremely free free free free free.*
> *Should I be so happy?*
> *There is no common person.*
> *The big clock chimes – not the clock but Mind*
> *chimes. The universe itself chimes. There is*
> *neither Mind nor universe. Dong, dong, dong!*
> *I've totally disappeared. Buddha is!*

This is the good news: each of us is God, we *are* God. This perennial realization, far more than merely intellectual understanding (though this kind of understanding is a good start), was called *gnosis* by early Christian and Sufi mystics in the Christian and Islamic traditions, respectively; by the same term in the Jewish mystical tradition of Kabbalah; *samadhi* in the Hindu Vedanta tradition; and *satori* in Zen Buddhism. These terms are not identical and nor does Buddhism generally use the term "God." But the experiences are essentially the same, as is clear from reading the many accounts, talking to those who have experienced this realization, or, ideally, having one's own experiences. These words each have their own specific connotations in their own traditions. But they do all share the key feature of true knowledge of one's identity with God and everything else in the universe. This is, in a word, "God-realization."

The rest of this book fleshes out these bones, a mere skeleton in these short introductory chapters. While rational discussion can at best inspire intellectual understanding, to become a more integrated person we must do more. We must achieve a lived understanding, a visceral understanding. We must feel it in our head, gut, heart and bones. And this isn't easy. There are many paths to achieve this integrated understanding and it is up to each of us to decide what is our best path or paths. The paths to understanding are described in the Hindu and Buddhist traditions as yogas, and more generally described as "praxis" (practice). There are many paths to God, some involving service, others involving devotion, others involving pure intellect and yet others involving mixtures of these. They are not mutually exclusive. Every aspect of our life is praxis.

It is helpful for many of us, however, to start with the intellectual understanding. And this is what this book focuses on. Knowing that you are the universe, that you are God, should come as a welcome realization! It should lead to great comfort and great compassion for creation, which is you. It becomes very difficult to treat others badly, or to treat our natural environment badly, when we internalize the knowledge that we are all of it. How can we despoil our environment when we realize it is our body? How can we mistreat others when we realize they are different parts of us, looking back at us with another set of our own eyes? How can we not have sympathy for bad behavior when we know the pain that produced that behavior?

*Whoever knows thus, 'I am Brahman,'
becomes this all. Even the gods cannot
prevent his becoming thus, for he becomes
them.*

Brihadaranyaka Upanishad I.4.10 (*circa* 700
BCE)

Part II: Some Thoughts on Thinking

I offer below a brief overview of what I think are key considerations for creating and maintaining a rational spirituality, a spirituality and science that consist of a single "deep science," to use Ken Wilber's very apt phrase. The main points: we don't know what we don't know, so we can never claim completeness or finality for any theory; it is nevertheless useful to attempt to create rational systems while always remaining humble when faced with the eternal mystery of reality.

Chapter 6: We never know the full extent of what we don't know

We never know what we don't know. Or, to be entirely accurate, we never know the full extent of what we don't know. Donald Rumsfeld, not exactly a philosopher or spiritual teacher, got at least one thing right in his unfortunate stint as Defense Secretary under President George W. Bush. In one of his press briefings, he stated: "There are known knowns. These are things we know that we know. There are known unknowns. That is to say, there are things that we know we don't know. But there are also unknown unknowns. These are things we don't know we don't know." This is simply a paraphrase of this chapter's title.

The proverbial tale of three blind men encountering an elephant is helpful for illustrating this truth. The first man (all of whom have been blind from birth) reaches for the elephant, to better understand its nature, and finds the elephant's trunk. "Clearly the elephant is long and slender like a snake." The second man reaches out and grasps the elephant's ear: "You've got it all wrong. This elephant is wide, thin and flat like a fan" The third man reaches out and grasps the elephant's tusk: "You've both got it wrong. This elephant is smooth, hard and long, like a spear." Those of us gifted with sight know that the elephant is all of these things. These are all aspects of the same creature. We can take the metaphor even further, however, when we realize that the blind men have no idea whether there is a tiger, or a snake, a tree, a book, or what have you, lying near the elephant. They cannot scan the landscape with their eyes and quickly gain an understanding of what is there.

The gift of sight is, however, a double-edged sword: its power often makes us forget that just as the blind men are limited by their senses, so we are limited by ours. Sight is but one way of perceiving the world. It is by no means the whole story. We enjoy, traditionally, five senses: sight, hearing, touch, taste and smell. These senses are all in fact different ways of perceiving electromagnetic forces, the most prominent of which is visible light. Our perceived world is a world of electromagnetism. But this is not the whole story either. We know from our technologically-augmented senses, the various tools that expand our natural senses, such as telescopes, microscopes and x-ray machines, that the part of the electromagnetic spectrum that we perceive with our eyes – visible light – is a tiny sliver of this spectrum. The broader spectrum includes radio waves, microwaves, x-rays and gamma rays, among other things. Electromagnetism also includes the electrostatic forces that hold our cells and molecules together. Without electromagnetism we wouldn't be able to perceive anything with our current senses and we wouldn't even have any senses because our bodies would simply fall apart without the binding force of electromagnetism.

There are at least three other forces at play in the universe: gravity, and the strong and weak nuclear forces. We perceive these forces indirectly because electromagnetic perceptions intervene. Last, we have very little reason to believe that these are the only forces at play: there is very strong evidence for at least one other force, which is responsible for "quantum entanglement." Quantum entanglement, also known as non-locality, refers to the fact that spatially separated particles display a clear link that apparently is transmitted faster than the speed of light. The speed of light is thought to be an absolute and universal speed limit for all real things. Entanglement has, however, been established over the last three decades with incontrovertible empirical evidence. Quantum entanglement is now a major impetus for an ongoing revision in how we view the universe and in our major physical theories, including the special and general theories of relativity. Combining quantum mechanics with general relativity is known as "quantum gravity" and finding a good theory of quantum gravity is considered to be one of the biggest challenges in modern physics.

The number of forces accepted by physics has changed considerably in the last century. In the 19th Century, electromagnetism and gravity were thought to be the only two forces. In the first half of the 20th century, the strong and weak nuclear forces were added to this repertoire. The strong force is responsible for holding the particles of the nucleus of an atom together. The weak force is responsible for radioactivity (to put it simplistically). More recently, herculean efforts have been expended in trying to reduce the number of forces back to one, in an effort known as "grand unification theory" or a "theory of everything." Physicists have succeeded in showing that electromagnetism and the strong and weak nuclear forces are manifestations of the same underlying phenomenon. It's just a matter of temperature – as temperatures rise extremely high, such as in the early history of our current universe, these forces collapse into one force. Or, more accurately, as temperatures dropped with the evolution of the universe, this one force, known as the "electro-weak force," separated into ostensibly different forces. The ongoing difficulty, thought by physicists to be perhaps the major problem in modern physics, as described by Lee Smolin in his masterful 2006 book *The Trouble With Physics*, is integrating gravity into the same mathematical framework as the other forces. This particular problem is accurately described, as mentioned above, as the problem of quantum gravity. More on these issues in later chapters.

History is, as always, helpful for shedding some light on today's physics. In a very illuminating passage about meteorites – objects falling from space to Earth – we see the hubris that is present in all ages with respect to the prevailing understanding of nature at that time:

> During the period of vigorous scientific

development which took place during the eighteenth century, scientists came to the conclusion that the falling of meteorites upon the Earth is impossible; all reports of such cases were declared to be absurd fiction. Thus, for example ... the Swiss mineralogist J.A. Deluc stated that 'if he saw a fall of a meteorite himself, he would not believe his own eyes.' But especially astonishing is the fact that even the well-known chemist Lavoisier signed a memorandum in 1772 with scientists of the Paris Academy of Sciences, which concluded ... that 'the falling of stones from the sky is physically impossible.' Finally, when the meteorite Barbotan fell in France in 1790 and the fall was witnessed by the mayor and the city council, the French scientist Berthollet wrote: 'How sad it is that the entire municipality enters folk tales upon an official record, presenting them as something actually seen, while they cannot be explained by physics nor by anything reasonable.'

Similarly, Lord Kelvin, a 19th Century British physicist who made major contributions to the study of electricity and thermodynamics, stated in 1900 that modern physics was all but complete: "There is nothing new to be discovered in physics now. All that remains is more and more precise measurement." His statement was spectacularly poorly timed because it was in the early years of the 20th Century that the two pillars of modern physics were developed: quantum mechanics and Einstein's relativity theories. As we shall see in later chapters there are ongoing difficulties with these two pillars that suggest these are not by any means the final answers either.

This is the briefest overview of just one area of science, albeit a highly fundamental and important area. Even this brief overview shows, however, that as our knowledge of the universe grows exponentially, we have no reason to believe that we will ever know the full extent of how it works, what forces are in effect at which temporal and spatial scales, or whether there are things we cannot even conceive of at this time that are key to a more accurate understanding of the universe. Richard Feynman, a 20th Century American Nobel Prize-winning physicist, reminded us that "even those ideas which have been held for a very long time and which have been very accurately verified might be wrong …. [W]e now have a much more humble point of view of our physical laws – everything *can* be wrong!"

These truths lead to a great humility and wonder: we will never know the full extent of what we don't know. Mystery shall thus always be a part of our universe. We should be forever humble in the face of mystery and not get too hung up on how much we think we know, individually or collectively. We have barely begun to scratch the surface and we have a great adventure ahead of us.

You suppose that I contemplate my life's work with calm satisfaction. But from nearby it looks very different. There is not one single notion that I am convinced will hold its ground and broadly speaking I am not certain of being on the right path

Albert Einstein, 1949, toward the end of his career

Chapter 7: It is helpful to believe that the universe is a rational place

Despite the undeniable fact that we shall never know the full extent of what we don't know – and can thus never state with certainty that a particular theory is complete or final – it is nevertheless *helpful* to believe that the universe is a rational place. The obvious evidence for believing that the universe does operate by discernible rules, which we are tempted to call laws when very reliable and sustained evidence supports their existence, is the ongoing march of technology. Perpetually shrinking phones and music machines, space travel, photos of distant nebulas, prosthetic devices that connect directly to one's brain, nuclear fission and fusion, panels that turn sunlight directly into electricity, and countless other inventions, are direct support for our ever-increasing understanding of the universe. More generally, our ability to gather data about the universe, expanding our horizons with each new discovery, suggests that we're onto something with this whole science and technology thing.

Modern science has, usually without stating this explicitly, examined the universe under the hypothesis that it is a rational place. This hypothesis has been supported abundantly thus far. But as with all hypotheses and theories it can never be proven, only probed and supported.

The system I advocate in this book is indeed a rational system, which also presupposes that the universe is a rational place. Acknowledging, however, that this is merely a hypothesis that may lead to useful results helps preserve our humility and the mystery inherent in the universe. The discerning reader will wonder at this point what "rational" means. This is the topic of the next chapter.

Chapter 8: The fundamental rule of reason is non-contradiction

Like many common terms, it's a lot more difficult than one would think at first to establish what "reason," "rational" or "reasonable" actually mean. "Reason" is probably the easiest term of these three to define so let's start there. "Reason" may be defined as the attempt to arrive at an understanding of various aspects of the universe by starting with first principles and making inferences based on those principles. Under this definition, two immediate additional questions arise: how are first principles established and how do we make valid inferences?

Ultimately, first principles are a matter of intuition. Another name for intuition is "induction," though this has a more precise meaning than intuition. Induction is the framing of general conclusions based on initial observations. Inductive thinking makes conclusions about a whole class of objects based on its observed particulars. We observe that birds have feathers and wings. We inductively hypothesize that all birds have feathers and wings. As far as we know to date, despite the presence of flightless birds like penguins and ostriches, all birds do indeed have feathers and wings. Yet we cannot rule out the possibility that we will find one day a creature that doesn't have feathers or wings that we are compelled for other reasons to classify as a bird.

Intuition and induction take the raw data of our senses and make provisional conclusions – hypotheses – about these data. Intuition and induction are highly dependent on taste and personal aesthetics. These issues of intuition and induction are generally unexamined when looking at broad areas of human inquiry such as science or spirituality. The undeniable truth is, however, that every field of human inquiry proceeds based on implicit or explicit first principles, and these first principles are to some degree always arbitrary because they are based on intuition and induction.

Based on first principles, which are proffered based on intuition and induction, we attempt to make valid inferences to come to further conclusions about whatever issue we are examining. This is where *deduction* comes in, another type of logic. Deduction proceeds in the opposite direction as induction. It makes specific conclusions based on data and generalities often called "premises."

This is an area discussed by philosophers at least as far back as the early Greeks and examined in detail by Aristotle in his *Metaphysics* and other works. Aristotle pointed out that the most basic rule of logic is non-contradiction. He called this the "principle of non-contradiction." This principle may be stated simply as: Something cannot be A and *not-A* at the same time. Another way of stating it: We cannot validly infer something that directly contradicts another valid inference. If we do, the whole system falls like a house of cards because we have no method for choosing between various possible inferences resulting from our assumptions/principles.

We see that the principle of non-contradiction is, as the name would suggest, both a first principle *and* a rule for how we make valid inferences from first principles. It is perhaps unique in this regard in that one can start with this single principle and construct a valid metaphysical and scientific system from this single building block. But as with all first principles, it is a matter of intuition and induction as to what is chosen as a first principle. Aristotle considered this to be the most firm of first principles and I would agree. But I also have to acknowledge that it isn't *necessarily* true as a principle. By definition, it can't be validated because it's a first principle. As discussed above, the view that the universe is a rational place is itself a hypothesis that may not ultimately be valid. It is, however, helpful to believe that it is a rational place and I choose, through intuition and induction, to start with the principle of non-contradiction as my first and most solid building block in constructing a rational edifice. By induction, I arrive at a system of valid deduction.

Accepting this as a starting point, we see quickly that self-contradiction, also known as "paradox," is a sure sign that a given hypothesis or theory has problems. It is surprising how often scientists and philosophers will discuss with interest various paradoxes in mainstream physics or philosophy, without realizing that under the first principle implicit in modern science, which developed from Aristotle through to the present day, such paradoxes are highly problematic. A paradox is a good sign that something is seriously awry with a theory.

A quick example: the most common interpretation of quantum mechanics is still (arguably) the Copenhagen interpretation developed by Niels Bohr, Werner Heisenberg, and Wolfgang Pauli, and many others in the 1920s and 30s. In this interpretation, based on copious experimental data, the fundamental constituents of matter and energy are thought to be both wave and particle at the same time, but these features manifest more overtly in different experimental and real world situations. Under the principle of non-contradiction, however, an object cannot be a wave and particle at the same time because to be a wave prevents the object in question from also being a "not-wave," which is anything other than a wave. And to be a particle prevents the object at issue from being at the same time a "not-particle," which is anything other than a particle. Hence the contradiction. Some interpretations of quantum mechanics resolve this apparent contradiction (the Bohmian interpretation, for example, after David Bohm) by suggesting that there is in fact both a particle and a wave, but the wave is part of the ever-present web of potentiality that produces our universe and the particle is the physical manifestation of that potentiality at that particular slice of space and time, akin to a small boat (particle) riding a stormy ocean (wave).

Chapter 9: Language and concepts are tools, not ends in themselves

Zen Buddhism is famous for being screwy and inscrutable. Yet much of its reputation comes from a very intentional playfulness with concepts of rationality, as well a broader very valid point about the nature of language and the nature of reality. One of the most basic insights of Zen – if we may use imperfect language to try and express this truth – is that concepts and language themselves are the source of abundant ongoing confusion. Concepts and language can never fully describe reality itself, the essence, the "thing in itself." Rather, at best, concepts and language can *point* to the underlying reality. Reality is reality and language is language. But language is part of reality and a key part of our heritage as human beings. Language should never be confused with reality itself. Thus, much of Zen's techniques are described as "direct pointing," as opposed to verbal techniques. Some direct pointing techniques involve language while many don't.

Alan Watts recounts a humorous example of Zen's direct pointing. A young monk is training with his colleagues and is consistently flummoxed by the seemingly inane answers the masters expect as a response to their mind-twisting questions. A well-known teaching tool in Buddhism is the *koan*, a seemingly paradoxical or non-sensical question. The most well-known koan asks "what is the sound of one hand clapping?" This is one of many techniques used to show the failure of language and logical thought and to point toward a deeper level of existence. In this particular teaching story recounted by Watts, the young monk, walking near his monastery one morning, comes across a cheerful frog. Seeing an opportunity, the monk scoops up the frog and hides it in his sleeve. Later that day, when asked to show the master his "true nature," the young monk quickly procures the frog from his sleeve and displays it proudly to his master. "Too intellectual!" was the immediate reply of the master.

As we will see time and time again, much confusion arises from choice of language, otherwise known as terminology. But when we boil terminology from various philosophical, scientific and spiritual traditions down to their essence, much of this confusion melts away. We find in many cases that different terms are pointing to the same feature of reality, but we are still enriched by following and understanding the various threads that point to the underlying reality.

While I agree with the Zen Buddhist "point" that language and logical thought ultimately fail us, there is obviously much utility in attempting to create rational models of the universe for more mundane purposes such as improving our medical science, traveling to distant planets, or simply building a car that runs on electricity, to list just a few examples. I also believe that it is helpful to approach spirituality from a rational perspective, while always maintaining that humility and recognition of mystery that spring from the most fundamental acceptance that we can never know the true nature of reality or find any firm validity in all of our efforts at rationalization. Language can point to direct pointing, so it indirectly helps us arrive at a deeper, non-language based, understanding of reality, the "thing in itself," or more accurately "the process in itself" since all things are processes, always changing.

We shall see in later chapters that many terms, such as "consciousness," "life," "energy," "information," "species," and the various difficult debates that arise from these concepts, have led to great confusion in our modern psyche. Much of this confusion may be eliminated by examining what these concepts point to and by the realization that these concepts don't point to any truly discrete "all or nothing" phenomena; rather, they point to various aspects of the constant flux that is part and parcel of the grand unity of the universe and of Source, the ocean of being.

Chapter 10: All knowledge is subjective

Cogito ergo sum. "I think, therefore I am." This is Descartes' famous statement that forms the basis for his rational system described in his *Principles of Philosophy* (1644). In this book, I adopt a slightly different version: "I experience, therefore experience exists." There is obviously some experience *here*, ostensibly behind my eyes. This undeniable conclusion (to me at least) leads *potentially* to Descartes' conclusion that there is also an "I." There must clearly be an *experiencer* to have any experience, but should we call this an "I"? The problem of the self, of "I-dentity," is a thorny briar that I introduced earlier and will dive into in later chapters.

For present purposes, it's important only to state that we can build our system on two first principles. We've already discussed one: the principle of non-contradiction. The second is that all knowledge is subjective. We can label this "the principle of necessary subjectivity." There is literally nothing that we know that isn't subjective because knowledge presupposes an experiencer, a subject.

We often talk about "objective knowledge" as though it is possible to skirt around the necessary subjectivity of all knowledge. Objective knowledge is not, however, incontrovertible and necessarily true. Rather, objective knowledge should be thought of as that knowledge that can be probed and supported by experiencers other than oneself. When I say the sky is blue, right here, right now, I can gain some confidence that this is a true statement because presumably anyone I ask around me would confirm that the sky is indeed blue. I could in fact ask this question of people around me if I seek confirmation of this statement. This means of establishing the alleged objectivity of knowledge is better described as "inter-subjective knowledge," however, because we can never know if the sky is really blue from all vantage points or even if the sky really exists "out there," as opposed to being a simulation or a dream. All we can do is make our own conclusions from our own particular first principles and then probe and hopefully support or negate our first principles through such probing. And this is the broader point that Descartes wished to make: the only thing we know to exist with certainty is that there is an experiencer. Everything else is supposition and conjecture.

A very practical and relevant consequence of the principle of necessary subjectivity is the acceptance of the validity of introspection as a tool for probing not only oneself but also the universe. Indeed, we realize that all probing is necessarily subjective because it's literally all right here in our heads. Even if we believe that there is a universe "out there," as I do for a variety of reasons, a philosophical position that makes me a type of "realist," we must also acknowledge that all information we have about the universe out there comes to us through our senses and intuitions and is, thus, right here in our heads. The introspective method has been downplayed in recent decades as an unreliable scientific method. But when we are being rigorous in our thinking we realize that all science, indeed all of human existence, is necessarily subjective. Science succeeds when each scientist's subjective experiences and intuitions are successfully passed to other subjective experiencers through discussion and the printed word. This is how science works, even when it's not commonly acknowledged that this is the case.

Chapter 11: Most things exist in degrees, not "all or nothing"

We, as human beings, biological forms, have evolved a way of perceiving and making sense of the world that relies on carving the world up into manageable chunks. This is, from an evolutionary perspective, inevitable and useful. How could complex forms like human beings have evolved without carving the world into perceptible chunks? We know from observing simpler life forms that perception comes in many types, most far less rich than human perceptions. A flatworm has an "eye" that detects only light and dark, as does the even simpler euglena, a single cell form of life. Similarly, examples abound of more rudimentary versions of what we call hearing, smell, touch and taste. Conversely, there are many examples of more advanced perception, such as a cat's ability to see in the dark, a dolphin's or a bat's echolocation, a shark's "lateral line" sense that allows it to detect electric fields in other animals, or some birds' ability to navigate long distances by using small amounts of magnetite, a mineral that reacts to the Earth's magnetic fields, in their bodies to align themselves with these fields.

All of our senses, and the senses of other creatures, evolved from simpler forms and consist of one essential function: gathering data about the world around us. This is indeed the definition of perception. Perception is simply reception of information. Our senses, to be useful in the grand game of evolution, had to present data to us and our innumerable forebears in digestible chunks. If it wasn't digestible, it wasn't useful, and thus would have no evolutionary value. So, in a way, our senses filter the vast array of possible information from the world around us into bite-size chunks that allow us to navigate our world without overwhelming us.

Now to the point of this chapter: this evolutionarily advantageous feature of our biological history can lead us astray when we are pondering many of the big questions tackled in this book. This is the case because we, by default, assume things around us to be "chunks," that is, all or nothing features of the world. This is a tendency that shows itself in us even at a very early age. Researchers have found that children as young as three behave very clearly as though they believe there is an "essence" of some sort in common objects around them. We even have this tendency toward "essentialism" (the more technical term for what I'm calling here "chunking") built into our biology in some manner. In short, essentialism, which is the opposite of a process view of reality, focuses on "things" as stable forms that have some kind of continuous identity. Process thought focuses on the change we observe in everything around us. All is process and what we think of in everyday life as things are actually processes.

A rock is perhaps our best example of a chunk, and it may be the basis for today's preference in thinking about the world as nothing but glorified billiard balls we call particles. There is obviously some utility in avoiding a falling rock or a tiger, and these are good examples of where chunking has been evolutionarily helpful. But is biological "life," as a concept, a chunk? Most of us think we know what "life" is, even if we couldn't offer an immediate definition. Life is, however, a classic example of something that is not a chunk. Life is, instead, a process that can be characterized by the various functions of eating, breathing, mating, birthing, fighting, etc. This means that life exists on a sliding scale; it's not all or nothing. In fact, no good *definition* of life, as opposed to *characterization*, is feasible because life is not a thing at all. As a *process*, we can characterize various sub-processes of what we call life. But as we'll see later, these characterizations all become a bit arbitrary.

All things in the universe are in fact processes, even such classic examples of "things" such as rocks. Whitehead highlighted this truth in his "process philosophy." His primary work in philosophy, published in 1929, is entitled *Process and Reality*. Process philosophy corrects the misunderstandings about reality that arise from those philosophies that focus on unchanging *substance*, on things. Process philosophy is the remedy for "substantialism," and today's materialism is an overly dogmatic form of substantialism. Today's substantialists and materialists often think of the world as nothing but tiny rocks, particles, billiard balls, even while they acknowledge that this is a highly outdated notion of reality given the developments of quantum mechanics and other areas of modern physics.

Another example of misplaced chunking is frequently found in discussions of consciousness. We all think we know what consciousness is, and indeed we do because we experience it directly. Experience is consciousness. Yet most of us would be hard-pressed to offer a definition of consciousness. This doesn't stop many, including the most sophisticated biologists and philosophers, from proposing various points in the history of life at which consciousness "emerges" from something that is thought to be non-conscious. In this theory, something we label consciousness appears where it did not exist before, in, as an example, a simple multi-cellular creature like a rotifer.

As we'll see later, establishing what we mean by our words is very important, but it is highly unlikely that there was any point at which consciousness emerged from what was not conscious in some manner already. Consciousness very likely goes all the way down and extends back to the beginning of time itself. Consciousness exists on a sliding scale, like life; it is not an all or nothing affair. In fact, some philosophers, such as Galen Strawson and David Ray Griffin, have argued that it is actually impossible for consciousness to "emerge" from what is not in some manner already conscious. How can an entirely new feature of the universe emerge from something that was entirely devoid of that same feature? This is a particularly difficult challenge for the "emergentist" camp of consciousness to explain.

Other examples of misplaced chunking include "species," which are always changing and never really definable; "planet" (remember the downgrade of Pluto from full planet status based on a reassessment of what constitutes a "planet"?); and human life itself, in terms of what constitutes a human being. This latter question is at the core of the always contentious right to choose/right to life debate surrounding the issue of abortion. We need not resolve these difficult questions here other than to note that they concern questions of practicality, not of deeper reality (ontology).

Is it practical to have a working understanding of what a species is? Of course. Field biologists and taxonomists would have a hard time doing their work without a working definition of species. Is it practical to have a working definition of what a planet is? Of course. Is it practical to have a working definition of when human life begins? Resoundingly yes, for obvious reasons. But in addressing the larger philosophical and spiritual issues that are the focus of this book – that can lead to an integrated science and spirituality and an integrated self – we need to peer below the level of practicality. We need to push aside the curtains of the "common sense" world created by our brain, and its eons-long evolutionary heritage, and see what lies behind the curtains. Or we must at least try to do so, insofar as we can, given the reality that we are evolved biological beings, with all the limitations that this entails.

Once we establish a deeper understanding, including the knowledge that most things in the universe aren't "chunks," we will return again to the level of practicality in later chapters. This return to practicality will be immeasurably aided by our deeper understanding.

These last few chapters are, then, the tools we find in our toolbox. These tools, like everything else, reside in our heads. In the grand effort to integrate ourselves, and to find an integrated view of science and spirituality, these tools can take us far toward the goal. But intellectual understanding is at best half the "battle." The other half, the more important half, is the lived understanding, the understanding in our gut and in our bones. Later chapters delve into ways to achieve a lived understanding. First we dwell a bit longer on how we can construct a rational science based on these building blocks. Parts III through VI describe what I believe is a self-consistent, scientifically and spiritually sound worldview. Part VII returns to practicality with suggestions for how we can live these understandings.

Part III: The nature of Nature

To be viable, any reconciliation between science and spirit must squarely address science itself. It cannot simply dismiss the conclusions of science where those conclusions contradict whatever spiritual view is preferred. For example, a thinking Christian shouldn't, if she considers herself guided by reason as well as faith, simply ignore Darwinian evolutionary theory because it contradicts the Biblical view. And a thinking Muslim shouldn't dismiss modern physics because it denies the reality of the soul. But nor should a person guided by both reason and faith take "on faith" the validity of today's prevailing scientific theories. To reconcile science and spirit, we must use the same "deep science" techniques in both science and spirituality.

Fortunately, there is no necessary contradiction between science and a spiritual view of the world. There are indeed many contradictions of specific outdated religious or spiritual views *vis a vis* today's scientific worldview. But the rational spirituality advocated here is based on a philosophical and scientific basis that no reasonable person should easily dismiss. Indeed, I believe that the scientific view of reality described in this Part is a more rigorous view than many of the prevailing concepts in today's physics and philosophy. The deep science approach attempts to be more scientific than today's conventional scientific worldview, not less. I come to this conclusion because of my wide-ranging examination of biology, physics, spirituality, politics and philosophy. In weaving together a single coherent worldview, which I have attempted, many of the contradictions and paradoxes of some of today's prevailing scientific theories are made evident. At the same time, the path toward an integrated worldview, incorporating the best of both science and spirituality, is made clear.

One or Many? Duality or non-duality? What is the ultimate nature of Nature? This is the oldest of philosophical questions, with direct relevance to broader scientific and spiritual concerns.

There certainly *seems* to be more than just "one thing" in our existence. There *is* an apparent multiplicity, an apparent rich diversity. When I look around I can't help but behold and enjoy the beauty of the multiplicity, such as the sky, cars, buildings, tables, people, animals, all sorts of activity, all around me. But what is this multiplicity at its *fundamental* level? What does it rest on? This is the root question behind the eons-long debate about the One and the Many, which goes back to the pre-Socratic Greek philosophers and the Hindu rishis, and probably much earlier. In other words, what is everything ultimately made of? One "stuff," two, or more?

It seems that all human cultures began with a polytheistic worldview, a story of the universe that included many different spirits and gods causing the many events, good and bad, that befell early humans who struggled to make sense of it all. This worldview makes some sense when we consider the evolution of consciousness from its earliest biological forms through pre-human animals and onward toward more human forms. Biological life necessarily entails some degree of competition because of scarce resources. The dawning of complex consciousness in our pre-human forebears, resulting from this competition for limited resources, can't have included an immediate realization that the world of our senses is as much illusion as reality, a suggestion of the deeper reality that lies behind it. The earliest philosophers and mystics, playing with pre-linguistic expression and eventually full-blown language, surely must have tried to make sense of the apparent multiplicity around us by positing various agents ("gods") behind the key themes observed as events unfolded around them. Over time, however, this early worldview shifted to monotheism and philosophical "monism." Monism is simply the view that all things in our universe are fundamentally one thing, one stuff. This worldview sees the obvious multiplicity but realizes, intuitively and/or deductively, that this multiplicity is not the full story – there is just one thing that somehow manifests the apparent multiplicity.

"Dualism," on the other hand, is the view that there are two fundamental substances, often described as matter and soul or the physical and the spiritual. There are of course many other philosophical positions regarding the ultimate nature of reality, an area of philosophy known as *ontology* or *metaphysics*, but we need not be exhaustive here.

The two centers of ancient civilization that seem to have been first to make the leap from pre-rational thinking to abstract philosophical thought, the eastern Mediterranean (including Greece and Egypt) and the Indian subcontinent, both seem to have undergone the transformation from polytheism to monotheism and/or philosophical monism within a few hundred years of each other. Thomas McEvilley, an American scholar of ancient thought, has traced this very interesting history in his masterful *The Shape of Ancient Thought: Comparative Studies in Ancient Greek and Indian Philosophies* (2002). He makes a compelling case that the pre-Socratic philosophers, Plato, Aristotle, and the neo-Platonic vision of Plotinus and other Western philosophers between the 5th Century BCE and 3rd Century CE, were heavily influenced by the Upanishadic tradition, one of the more prominent schools of Hindu philosophy. The influence surely went both ways, however, and we shall never know the full extent of this cross-fertilization.

This Eastern influence on Western thought was generally described as an "Oriental" influence on western philosophy that resulted in "orientalized" philosophies. The shift from the polytheism of the Hindu Vedas, the earliest writings in India, which date back to about 1500 BCE, to the philosophical monism of Upanishadic philosophy took about seven hundred years. It only took about two hundred years for the Greek culture to make a similar shift. To McEvilley, this suggests, along with many other fairly compelling lines of evidence, including remarkably detailed similarities in various texts and concepts, that there was significant cross-fertilization between the Indian and Mediterranean cultures.

I have already provided an argument for non-duality (philosophical monism) in earlier chapters. In its simplest form, this argument rests on the realization that to "be in the universe" means all objects must be connected, directly or indirectly, to all other objects; thus, the universe consists of a single unbroken web of interconnections. We are part of that web, an inseparable piece of the universe. We are, thus, at our deepest level the entire universe because if the universe cannot be separated into its parts, each ostensible part is also the whole. The "ostensible" in the previous sentence is key because the apparent separation is just that: apparent. This is the basis for the *gnosis* experience common to almost all spiritual traditions.

Yet there is an undeniable duality built into the universe. The universe is, for each of us, split into "self" and "other," between our own self and the rest of the universe. Even if this duality is "ostensible," how does it arise and if it is mere appearance why is this mere appearance so compelling? In other words, how do we explain non-duality in light of the clear duality in our actual experience?

To be a subject requires some kind of separation. There is, then, *some* degree of separation between our self and the universe. The phrase "some degree" in the previous sentence is, however, very important. There is a split between self/other, subject/object, knower/known, in each of us and in each subject throughout the entire universe. How can this split be reconciled with non-duality? The reconciliation arises from the recognition that this split, while real from a personal perspective, is not a fundamental split. It does not go to the very foundation of reality. At the foundation of reality, all things are One. The One is Brahman, which is pure being, pure Source, and thus not conscious. There is no duality within Brahman because Brahman is literally everything. Duality thus rides on the back of non-duality. Duality is not fundamental; non-duality is fundamental.

The split *seems* fundamental only when we confine our gaze to the phenomenal realm, the realm of the shadows in Plato's cave. When we look deeper, to the realm of Source/Brahman/ether/ocean of being, we see that there cannot be anything other than unity in this more fundamental realm. This fundamental unity is the light itself, the sun, in Plato's cave allegory. This is the realm that combines subject and object. Indeed, at this level there is no subject, no object, just pure Spirit that is beyond the subject/object distinction. This is the case because if Brahman is literally everything, how can there be any object for it to perceive? It is everything; there is nothing outside of it.

It is only through the emanations of Brahman that constitute the physical/phenomenal realm that the actual universe is made real, that the multiplicitous universe of experience arises. This multiplicity is known as *maya* in the

Vedanta tradition. Maya is the world of phenomena. When Brahman dreams and produces the wonderful universe of *maya*, it is this upwelling of Spirit, of pure being, and only this, that leads to the separation of object and subject, to experience. Experience requires this split between object and subject. Experience *is* the separation between object and subject, with a link between the two. Without this separation, there is only *Om*. Om is the preferred transcendent reality. Om is *what it is like to be Brahman*, but we, as conscious beings, can't exist in Om perpetually. These transcendent states of non-separation are always fleeting and beyond full recollection when we return to more normal states of consciousness. This return leaves residual bliss in its wake. This is, again, the *gnosis/Samadhi/satori* experience. (I'll use "gnosis" from now on to describe this experience, not because of my preference for the Greek/Christian tradition, but largely because I just like the look and feel of this word).

Does this mean that our subjectivity, the split between subject and object, is an illusion? No. This split is real insofar as there is experience, here, now, in me, and in all other experiencers. Consciousness is real. But this split melts away into non-duality when we plumb the depths of reality, when we dive deeply into Source. The key feature of *gnosis*, alluded to in previous chapters, is the disappearance of subjectivity and an undeniable feeling of union with the universe. The ego dissolves during this blissful condition as we realize our true universal and divine identity. Indeed, Vedanta philosophy, the philosophy contained in the Upanishads, describes Brahman, the fundamental non-dual reality that sustains the phenomenal world, as *satcitananda*: being, knowledge, bliss. Brahman is that. This deepest level of reality is, thus, not conscious – it is Brahman's emanations that give rise to consciousness. Brahman itself is not conscious. It is pure being rising into consciousness as its emanations rise into actuality.

When we experience Brahman directly during *gnosis/samadhi/satori*, we realize pure bliss and experience the fact that we are the entire universe. We are awakened to our true nature. We come back and remember what happened, including the dissolution of ego, of self, and we are provided additional clues as to the true nature of Nature. These clues help us return to the bliss of non-duality and to rely on those memories to sustain us in this world of duality.

This truth is the basis, then, for both a rich spirituality and, as we shall see now, a rigorous scientific framework. Non-duality is the ultimate reality and everything else flows from it. Duality rides on the back of non-duality.

Chapter 13: Space is not empty

We take philosophical monism – non-duality – described in the previous chapter, as our starting point for building a rational spirituality. To build the science of our philosophical monism we must examine the features of our perceived reality and explain how they fit with each other. Space is one of the fundamental ideas, but is it really fundamental? We shall see, terminology aside, that space is not a truly fundamental concept.

Is space just an empty container for matter? Or is it something much more? A thought experiment is revealing. Imagine you are on a roller coaster. You start moving slowly as it leaves the loading dock. You know you are moving at first simply because you see the coaster leaving the dock, with you as its passenger. You don't feel much at first. As the coaster climbs the first steep slope, you feel gravity pulling back on you as your body reclines on the upward ride. You return to an upright position as you reach the crest, slow, and then scream as you and the rest of the thrill-seekers descend down the first horrific slope. You feel the force of acceleration in your face, in your limbs and your behind. As the coaster reaches the bottom it whips to the right around the first bend and your body is pressed hard against the left side of the car. The coaster whips left around the second bend and your body is pressed hard against your friend next to you on the right. You go through this many times and finally return to the dock, emotionally exhausted and wondering why you ever signed up for such a "fun" ride.

Now, what is it that caused your body to move around as the coaster moved around? Most people will quickly answer "inertia." Inertia is a name for the fact that solid bodies resist acceleration, which is any change in velocity. In other words, solid things like to be left alone and don't change unless they are disturbed. "Inertia" is a good answer, but it raises the question: what is inertia? Why did your body feel the motion like it did and why do solid things resist acceleration more generally, as the concept of inertia suggests they do? It may surprise the reader to learn that this is in fact a very open question in physics. Physics has given the name inertia to this phenomenon and it has been studied in detail at least since the time of Galileo. Inertia presupposes the presence of "mass," a key feature of what physicists generally call "matter." What is mass? Mass is what is affected by gravity, and mass in turn exerts gravitational force on other mass. Why does mass react to gravity? The Higgs field, discovered in 2012 and leading to the Nobel Prize in physics in 2013, is thought to be the physical basis for mass.

There is some debate about the validity of the data behind the discovery of the Higgs field and time will tell how well this discovery holds up. The Higgs field, however, supports the assertion that inertia is a property of space itself. This is the case because the Higgs field becomes the stuff of space itself, under some interpretations. Space is not empty. It has certain properties, one of which is the ability to make matter resistant to acceleration: inertia.

Every physical theory has two key components: the mathematical formalisms and the interpretation of the formalisms. While today's Standard Model of particle physics, based on quantum mechanics, has been found to be incredibly accurate in terms of its mathematical formalisms, and the predictions they afford, the interpretation of the symbols in the equations (the formalisms) remains highly problematic. This is quickly made apparent by a review of the dozens of competing interpretations offered by various physicists since quantum theory was first developed in the early part of the 20th Century. The details of this discussion are beyond the scope of this book, but I feel the coming decades will yield significant progress in interpreting the deep nature of reality. Regardless of the ultimate validity of the Standard Model and its interpretation, my key point here remains valid: empty space is not really empty because it has many properties that demonstrate the existence of something beyond ostensibly "empty" space.

This is not a controversial perspective at this time, as many physicists and philosophers have realized that the traditional notion of space as empty is outdated. Stephen Hawking states that "gravity gives rise to the structure of space itself. To put this plainly, gravity is defined even in 'empty' space, and thus, there must be something" even in empty space. He adds: "That 'something' is the ether, or, in modern language, a field... In the modern view, all forces arise from fields. In quantum theory... the particles themselves arise from the field."

So: space is not empty. There is structure to space, deeper levels of reality that science is only now plumbing.

This scientific discussion will become relevant to our spiritual inquiries in future chapters, as I attempt to meld physical and scientific theories about the nature of space with spiritual theories about the ultimate nature of reality.

We must keep in mind that there is an inherent risk in using modern science to support alleged spiritual truths because science is always changing. A key strength of the "deep science" approach I pursue in this book, however, is that both spiritual and scientific endeavors rely on constant experimentation and re-evaluation. Spiritual and scientific truths can and should constantly evolve as we learn more about our infinitely complex and exciting universe. We are not, under this approach, writing anything in stone, whether scientific or spiritual truths.

The term "ether" is unique in the history of physics not only because of the so many different meanings in which it has been used but also because it is the only term that has been eliminated and subsequently reinstated, though with a different connotation, by one and the same physicist [Einstein].

Max Jammer, in the Foreword to *Einstein and the Ether* (2000)

Chapter 14: The ocean of being supports reality in each moment

Modern physics contains many dramas. It is unfortunate that these dramas are not better-known outside of the physics or philosophy of physics communities because they are very telling about the personalities in this most respected of sciences. They also illuminate the limitations of modern science – indeed, of all science. A particularly interesting drama is the story of the "ether," a story that has unfolded over the course of many thousands of years.

The ether is the comeback kid of physics. Over the last two centuries, the concept has fallen in and out of vogue, in various versions, but it appears to be on the comeback again in the opening years of the 21st Century, as the Hawking quote in the last chapter suggests. The modern concept of the ether is a field or set of fields comprising fundamental reality – often described as the Higgs field or the Higgs condensate, which we have touched on in previous chapters. Modern science has, then, come full circle with respect to the ether, perhaps more than once.

The ancient Greek "pre-Socratic" philosophers, so-named because they lived before Socrates, were perhaps the first to theorize about the ether, as a "fifth element" in addition to the accepted elements of air, earth, water and fire. The term "quintessential" refers to this original notion of the ether.

In Eastern philosophy, particularly in the Hindu tradition, the conceptual equivalent to the ether is either Brahman, the ocean of being, or *Akasha* or the *Akashic field* (depending on what specific tradition we draw from). The Akashic field is both the ocean of being and the repository of all information in the universe, preserving in some manner all that has ever happened in its infinite memory store.

The "luminiferous ether" was a 19th Century revival of certain aspects of the ancient ether, and was widely discussed with respect to the "wave theory of light." If light consists of waves, as was widely believed at the time, the ether was posited as the medium through which these waves moved, just as water waves move through the medium of the ocean. Until, that is, Einstein came along and made his own waves by dismissing the ether from mainstream physics in his famous 1905 paper on special relativity.

Einstein's views on the ether changed dramatically throughout the course of his career. His 1905 paper boldly proclaimed the ether to be a "superfluous" concept. At the time of Einstein's writing, the ether was thought to be both a medium through which light traveled and the basis of a universal frame of reference ("absolute space," to use Newton's term). Einstein's objective in developing special relativity was to extend earlier notions of relativity, which concerned only gravity, to electromagnetism – the second force that was formalized in the mid-19th Century by

Faraday, Maxwell and many others – thereby eliminating the need for a universal, "privileged," frame of reference in the realms of both gravity and electromagnetism. This approach, Einstein thought, would return modern physics to a fundamental symmetry that is considered particularly beautiful and useful by physicists.

A frame of reference is a mathematical coordinate system that allows an observer to map the features of the universe around her in relation to each other. The most well-known coordinate system we use today is the Cartesian system of x and y axes that every math student learns in middle school. The 0,0 origin of the coordinate system acts as the origin for any particular frame of reference. For any set of real world phenomena we can arbitrarily choose an origin as the basis for our particular frame of reference and then describe literally everything else in relation to the chosen origin. But is there an "absolute" frame of reference that is "correct"? The "relativity" in relativity theory means that any frame of reference is as good as any other in describing physical phenomena. There is no "correct" or universal frame of reference in relativity theory.

The classic example of pre-Einstein versions of relativity theory (known as either "Galilean" or "Newtonian" relativity) is a moving ship. To an observer on the moving ship, all things on the ship move at the same rate and the moving ship is itself the appropriate origin for a sailor's frame of reference. To an observer on shore alongside the moving ship, however, the land itself, *terra firma*, is the more appropriate frame of reference. A cannon ball rolling along the deck of the moving ship will be judged to be moving at different speeds from the point of view of these two observers. But neither point of view is "wrong." They're both correct, but "relative." This is the case because either frame of reference can adequately describe any given phenomena; and different frames of reference can easily be transformed into the other merely by adding or subtracting the appropriate numbers.

With Einstein's extension of relativity theory to include electromagnetism as well as gravity, there is no need to worry about what is the "correct" or truly stationary frame of reference for either gravity or electromagnetism, the two forces known at the time Einstein developed his theory in 1905 (we are now up to at least four forces when we include the strong and weak nuclear forces). While Einstein's relativity theory, with its rejection of an ether of any sort, obviously can be very useful and potentially simpler than alternatives, Einstein's own thinking evolved to the point that he realized that some type of ether was theoretically necessary after all – but not as a universal frame of reference. Rather, Einstein came to realize that the ether was necessary to explain various properties of space, such as inertia. The "ether" was, for the later Einstein, simply a term that describes the properties of space. It is not a separate substance, as was the case for earlier notions of the ether. It is, instead, space itself, but that space is not empty: it has certain qualities that manifest physically.

In 1915, Einstein published his paper on the general theory of relativity, which asserted a very different conception of space and time than his earlier special theory of relativity published in 1905, which had rejected the ether as superfluous. In general relativity, space has no independent existence; rather, it is a consequence of the various fields that are considered to be more fundamental than space itself. Shortly after his momentous general relativity paper was published, he exchanged letters with Hendrik Lorentz, one of his mentors, on the topic of the ether. Lorentz, a Dutch physicist and Nobel Prize winner who was a slightly older contemporary of Einstein's, argued that some notion of the ether was necessary. Einstein conceded eventually, during the course of their discussions, that some type of ether was necessary to explain inertia and acceleration. Einstein called this concept the "new ether." Einstein realized that the force responsible for your body careening around in our hypothetical roller coaster applied to all objects and that it was a property of space itself. Einstein wrote in a 1919 letter to Lorentz:

> It would have been more correct if I had limited myself, in my earlier publications, to emphasizing only the non-existence of an ether velocity, instead of arguing the total non-existence of the ether, for I can see

that with the word *ether* we say nothing else than that space has to be viewed as a carrier of physical qualities.

From 1916 to 1918, Einstein was in the thick of discussions with a number of colleagues about the nature of space and the ether, with respect to general relativity. As Walter Isaacson recounts in his wonderful biography of Einstein, *Einstein: His Life and Universe*, Einstein's thinking changed dramatically during this period. In 1920, Einstein became more emphatic regarding the ether, recognizing explicitly that the ether was a necessary medium by which acceleration and rotation may be judged, independently of any particular frame of reference:

> To deny ether is ultimately to assume that empty space has no physical qualities whatever. The fundamental facts of mechanics do not harmonize with this view... Besides observable objects, another thing, which is not perceptible, must be looked upon as real, *to enable acceleration or rotation to be looked upon as something real* ... The conception of the ether has again acquired an intelligible content, although this content differs widely from that of the ether of the mechanical wave theory of light ... According to the general theory of relativity, space is endowed with physical qualities; in this sense, there exists

an ether. Space without ether is
unthinkable; for in such space there not
only would be no propagation of light, but
also no possibility of existence for
standards of space and time.....

Einstein struggled with these ideas for much of his career.
The major conversion from the young Einstein of 1905 to
the mature Einstein of 1916 and later years reflected his
changing philosophical views regarding what can or cannot
be observed directly, and thus what can be said to exist or
not. Ernst Mach, the 19th Century German physicist and
philosopher, was a major influence on the young Einstein.
Mach believed strongly that if we can't measure something
directly or otherwise observe it directly then it may as well
not exist. This view is known generally as "positivism."
Einstein followed Mach's philosophy in his dismissal of the
ether as "superfluous" in his 1905 paper. As we've seen, he
later repudiated this view, realizing that the ether concept
is in fact necessary to explain the properties of space –
acceleration and rotation, at the least – despite the failure
of many experiments designed to find evidence of the
ether to actually find such evidence. Einstein thus
converted from a positivist in the tradition of Mach early in
his career, avoiding discussion of things that cannot be
seen or measured and thus to be considered outside the
purview of physics, into a true realist by the time he wrote
his 1916 paper on general relativity. As a realist, Einstein
argued during the middle and latter parts of his career that

physics must attempt to describe what is real and not avoid discussion of logically and physically necessary concepts, even if they cannot be directly detected – such as the ether.

Isaacson relates two very telling conversations between Einstein and his colleagues in the 1920s:

> "We cannot observe electron orbits inside the atom," Heisenberg said. "A good theory must be based on directly observable magnitudes."

> "But you don't seriously believe," Einstein protested, "that none but observable magnitudes must go into a physical theory?"

> "Isn't that precisely what you have done with relativity?" Heisenberg asked with some surprise.

> "Possibly I did use this kind of reasoning," Einstein admitted, "but it is nonsense all the same."

> In other words, Einstein's approach had evolved.

> Einstein had a similar conversation with his friend in Prague, Philipp Frank. "A

new fashion has arisen in physics," Einstein complained, which declares that certain things cannot be observed and therefore should not be ascribed reality.

"But the fashion you speak of," Frank protested, "was invented by you in 1905!"

Replied Einstein: "A good joke should not be repeated too often."

Isaacson adds, from a more intellectual perspective:

To a pure proponent of Mach, or for that matter of Hume [the Irish philosopher], the whole phrase "really to exist in nature" lacked clear meaning. In his special relativity theory, Einstein had avoided assuming the existence of such things as absolute time and absolute distance, because it seemed meaningless to say that they "really" existed in nature when they couldn't be observed. But henceforth, during the more than four decades in which he would express his discomfort with quantum theory, he increasingly sounded like a scientific realist, someone who believed that an underlying reality existed

in nature that was independent of our
ability to observe or measure it.

Einstein made this view explicit in a 1920 speech he gave at
the University of Leiden, Holland, where Lorentz taught:
"Besides observable objects, another thing, which is not
perceptible, must be looked upon as real [, the ether]...."
So for Einstein, even though the ether was considered at
the time to be undetectable, he deduced its existence
because of its effects on observable matter through
inertia, acceleration and rotation.

Einstein stated in his 1938 book, *The Evolution of Physics*:
"This word ether has changed its meaning many times in
the development of science. ... Its story, by no means
finished, is continued by the relativity theory."

Since 1938, the "ether" term has generally remained in
disfavor even as many discoveries have been found that
support strongly the notion that space is not empty. So
even while today's physicists rarely discuss the ether by
name, they discuss it by implication. Its most common
synonyms today are space-time or the vacuum. A notable
exception to the taboo against the "ether" terminology is
Nobel Prize winner Frank Wilczek's 2008 book, *The
Lightness of Being: Mass, Ether and the Unification of Forces*.
Wilczek writes: "Quite undeservedly, the ether has
acquired a bad name." Wilczek presents in his book a new
"unified field theory" that suggests the presence of an
ether that is a "superconducting supercollider."

To sum up, then, what is probably a confusing topic to those without a background in such matters: the ether is very much a necessary concept in modern physics, at least insofar as it is widely acknowledged that space has certain properties. The "ether" term is still not widely used and it will raise many eyebrows when it is discussed as a real feature of the universe. However, terminology aside, the idea that space has certain properties is a pervasive view among physicists and philosophers. Some well-known physicists have even begun to use the ether term again.

The ether, in the worldview I advocate in this book, gives rise to the various properties of space and is the ongoing source of creation for what we consider matter and energy. When we think deeply, we realize that this notion of the ether, from a physics perspective, begins to look a lot like the Source/ocean of being/Brahman that has traditionally been considered purely a spiritual or philosophical concept. Our theme of oneness and unification is thus moved one step further forward when we realize that philosophy, spirituality and physics arguably all share the key concept of Source/ocean of being/Brahman/ether.

Considered in its physical, concrete reality, the stuff of the universe cannot divide itself but, as a kind of gigantic "atom," it forms in its totality ... the only real indivisible.... The farther and more deeply we penetrate into matter, by means of increasingly powerful methods, the more we are confounded by the interdependence of its parts .... It is impossible to cut into this network, to isolate a portion without it becoming frayed and unraveled at all its edges.

20th Century French paleontologist and Jesuit priest Pierre Teilhard de Chardin,
The Phenomenon of Man (1959)

Chapter 15: Matter and energy are not as solid as they seem

Matter is the term modern physics uses to describe the apparent solidity of objects around us. What is a chair made of? It is made of various types of molecules – wood, fabric, steel, etc. – which are in turn comprised of atoms. Atoms are comprised of various sub-atomic particles, including electrons, neutrons and protons. These components have additional sub-components. Where this chain ends is also very much an open question in physics today. String theory is the most prominent effort in the early part of the 21st Century to describe the most fundamental constituents of matter – in this case, "strings." Strings are envisioned as extremely tiny loops of vibrating energy. In this theory, then, matter and energy are ultimately unified at the most fundamental level.

Considering matter and energy to be two aspects of the same stuff is a widespread view, held even by many scholars who don't necessarily subscribe to string theory as the final theory of everything. The most famous equation in all of physics, Einstein's $E = mc^2$, expresses very succinctly the equivalency of matter and energy. E is energy, m is mass and c is the speed of light. So energy equals mass times the speed of light squared. The speed of light is very fast, so a small amount of mass can produce a huge amount of energy. This, then, is the theoretical basis for nuclear fission, which can be used to produce electricity or to produce explosions (to put it very simply).

An interesting consequence of our ability to probe ever smaller scales of matter, from molecules to atoms, to subatomic particles and even further down in more limited ways, is the realization that there's really not much there. In other words, the more we drill down on what is behind the apparent solidity of objects around us the more we realize that solid things are overwhelmingly composed of empty space. The nucleus of an atom, when compared to the full atom, is equivalent in size to a grain of sand in the center of a sports stadium. It's tiny. And yet the large majority of all mass in an atom is contained in that tiny nucleus.

This puzzling feature of reality becomes even more puzzling when we take seriously the idea that matter and energy are equivalent. If this is the case, even that tiny nucleus at the center of each atom isn't "really" solid. It's just condensed energy of some sort, shimmering in space, but somehow containing the properties of the atom in question. This line of reasoning immediately raises the follow-up question: "what is energy?"

If we consider energy to be the most fundamental reality behind the apparent solidity of matter, it becomes very difficult to define what energy "really" is. Ultimately, this discussion becomes just a word game. We can define energy by using yet more words. But what we're trying to do is to explain the apparent solidity around us, the apparent solidity that our senses present to us. When we realize that this is the true objective, we also realize that it doesn't in the end matter what terms we use. We can label the apparent solidity around us "matter," as is the usual convention. Or we can label it "condensed energy," or we can use both terms. Or we can describe it as "really" tiny vibrating strings, when we look all the way down. We could even label the "true" reality behind our senses "Ideas," as Plato did and many Idealist philosophers since Plato have done. What really matters, however, is not the terminology but the conceptual placeholder. What are we trying to explain? In this case we're trying to explain the apparent solidity of the physical world.

Philosophers like Alfred North Whitehead and Arthur Koestler have realized this difficulty and have opted to use more general terms that will remain accurate and useful no matter what terms our current physical theories prefer. For Whitehead, a towering intellect active from about 1890 to the 1940s, at Cambridge University in England and later at Harvard, the ultimate constituents of reality are "events." An event is just another name, but it's very different than traditional views of "matter" or "energy." An event is a happening, a becoming. It requires some *process*, which we normally thing of as "things" (solidity) and some *duration* (time). So the event-based ontology is different conceptually than the traditional notions of matter or energy. An event never exists outside of time, by definition. Time – duration – is built into the definition. It is thus a more complete description of fundamental reality because it recognizes that no physical thing exists outside of time. All actual things, to *be* actual, which means they are perceivable or "physical," must exist in time. We can conceptually freeze objects. We can image an arrow frozen in mid-flight, hanging in space. But this is just a reflection of our imaginations, not a reflection of reality. Believing that actual things can in fact be frozen in time is a classic case of reification or what Whitehead calls the "fallacy of misplaced concreteness." Similarly, modern physics often imagines that the ultimate constituents of matter could in actuality be frozen in place and given a name, independent of time. Physics takes the approach of, to be a bit loose in my language, of asking the universe to "just please hold still for a second so that we can study you." But it never does. The universe is always in motion, always becoming. In reality, nothing is ever frozen in time. Time is always proceeding forward. It is, then, a mistake to conceptually separate matter from time and to believe that this conceptual separation is indicative of reality. Time is discussed further in the following chapter.

Arthur Koestler, a Hungarian philosopher and author with a huge range of interests, coined another term that is perhaps even more general than Whitehead's events. Koestler described a *holon* as a universal unit of organization that is both a part and a whole. Koestler writes:

A part, as we generally use the word, means something fragmentary and incomplete, which by itself would have no legitimate existence. On the other hand, there is a tendency among holists to use the word 'whole' or '*Gestalt*' as something complete in itself which needs no further explanation. But wholes and parts in this absolute sense do not exist anywhere, either in the domain of living organisms or of social organizations. What we find are intermediary structures on a series of levels in ascending order of complexity, each of which has two faces looking in opposite directions: the face turned toward the lower levels is that of an autonomous whole, the one turned upward that of a dependent part.

Koestler's holon is a very useful explanatory concept that can be used to describe any level of reality. It can also be used outside of physics to describe social organization or biological structures. For the rest of this book, I'll only use the term holon to describe physical – solid – structures. In wrapping up this chapter, which is admittedly rather dense for those readers not familiar with physics or philosophy, I want to close with my main point.

For Whitehead and Koestler, all events and all physical holons have an accompanying experience. Each event is, according to Whitehead, a "drop of experience." This is, again, panpsychism, a key concept discussed in earlier chapters. If all things are better described as events, then all things have experience. For these thinkers, experience goes all the way down. And up. We needn't take this view on faith. We can use reason to deduce this conclusion, as we did in earlier chapters. This is yet another step toward our integration of physical, philosophical and spiritual views. We are working our way toward a seamless and self-consistent model of physical and spiritual reality.

Rather than discrete things and independent events, there are but ripples upon ripples upon waves upon waves in this universe, propagating in a seamless sea.

20th Century Hungarian systems theorist and philosopher Ervin Laszlo

The ability of form to be active is the most characteristic feature of mind, and we have something that is mind-like already with the electron.

20th Century American physicist David Bohm

Chapter 16: Time is, time passes

We are as intimate with time as we are with our own experience, our own subjectivity. Yet the answer to the question: *what is time?* continues to evade a broad consensus. This is not surprising because most of the fundamental concepts discussed in the last few chapters have evaded such a consensus. And in areas where there *is* a fairly broad consensus, it is unsatisfactory for various reasons. The concept of time I describe here attempts to weave the concepts of time and free will into a coherent whole, along with the other physical concepts already discussed – and, of course, the view of consciousness described in earlier chapters.

Here is the short answer on the nature of time itself: time is simply change, process. Time is real, inescapable and passes in a necessary forward direction. Time is one aspect of the *creative advance*, the process by which the entire actual universe is created anew in every moment. Each instantiation of the present flows to the next instantiation, throughout the entire universe. As the creative advance works its magic, laying down the universe in each moment, time is what we call that process of changing moments.

Lee Smolin writes in his 2006 book *The Trouble With Physics* that "there is something basic we [physicists] are all missing, some wrong assumption we are all making."

Smolin ventures a guess as to what he and his fellow physicists have been missing:

> What could that wrong assumption be? My guess is that it involves two things: the foundations of quantum mechanics and the nature of time. ... But I strongly suspect that the key is time. More and more, I have the feeling that *quantum theory and general relativity are both deeply wrong about the nature of time*. It is not enough to combine them. There is a deeper problem, perhaps going back to the origin of physics.

I believe that Smolin is right about this basic mistake from the early days of physics and philosophy. Even though mainstream physics has yet to make the widely accepted breakthrough with respect to time that Smolin anticipates, some philosophers and physicists have over the last hundred years developed a notion of time that is the basis for some promising developments in physics. Smolin's 2013 book, *Time* Reborn, details Smolin's own views on the nature of time and a re-framing of modern physics that matches our common sense view of time as inherently real and not illusory. For the large majority of thinking people who are non-physicists, the philosophy of time I describe here provides some comfort that many of our intuitive notions about time and free will are, thankfully, not mere illusions.

Einstein, however, famously described time, the distinction between past, present and future, as a "stubbornly persistent illusion." His statement was prompted by his relativity theories, which consider time to be another dimension, like the more familiar three dimensions of space. Conceptualizing time as a dimension in this way leads to the idea that there is no necessary forward movement to time's arrow and that the universe could, in theory, evolve "backwards" in time just as well as going forward. A classic example of this counter-intuitive notion considers a breaking egg. In our normal universe, an egg falling from a kitchen counter to the floor will break into many pieces. A broken egg will never spontaneously gather its shards, white and egg together and re-coalesce back into a pristine egg. This reversal of time's arrow is not, however, forbidden by today's physics. It could, in theory, happen. This is counter-intuitive and, I believe, a mistaken notion that is based on mistaking Einstein's theories (and related physical theories) for statements about the *necessary* nature of reality.

When we consider the nature of reality more generally, keeping in mind the humility forced upon us by realizing that we shall never know the full extent of what we don't know, we may conclude that Einstein's relativity theories and related theories are useful in many ways but they do not provide the final word on the nature of reality. In other words, there is plenty of room to craft rigorous arguments for the reality of time by either reinterpreting relativity theory or by arguing directly against the validity of relativity theory. Einstein himself stated in 1949, toward the end of his illustrious career:

> You suppose that I contemplate my life's work with calm satisfaction. But from nearby it looks very different. There is not one single notion that I am convinced will hold its ground and broadly speaking I am not certain of being on the right path

The essence of why time is an "illusion" for Einstein relates to the initial assumptions in his theory of special relativity (which led to general relativity a decade later). This is, again, a fairly complicated history, but worth delving into here because of its huge importance in the mainstream materialist worldview. Einstein assumed, as a hypothesis based on a number of experiments that suggested the speed of light always remained constant, that the speed of light *was* in fact constant for all observers, regardless of what speed the observer was traveling. This assumption is very counter-intuitive when we compare it to our normal experience. In normal experience, an observer's speed is directly relevant to the relative speed of other things that are observed. When I drive to work alongside a speeding train, which is traveling at a constant speed, the speed of the train *in relation to me* in my car is highly dependent on the speed of my car. The train's speed in relation to my car does *not* remain the same no matter how hard I step on the gas. The train's relative speed changes as I go faster –

in fact, if it's initially traveling faster than I am, as I step on the gas I will eventually pull up alongside the train and be moving at the same speed as the train. If I keep on accelerating, I will eventually start moving past the train and it will recede into the distance behind me. But light doesn't work that way, or so Einstein postulated. No matter how fast I accelerate, the speed of light in relation to me will *always stay the same*. Nothing else in the universe behaves this way.

Ironically, in Einstein's relativity theories the only speed that is *not* relative is the speed of light. It's constant for all observers moving at whatever speed in relation to light or in relation to each other; the speed of light is absolute. If the speed of light is absolute everything else becomes relative, including space and time.

So why is light different? Einstein didn't address this philosophical point in his early work. Rather, he simply assumed (postulated) that light was different, as a working hypothesis to build a broader theory. What happens when we assume that light's speed is constant for all observers? Time and space become malleable, as opposed to the more intuitive "absolute time" and "absolute space," which were the prevailing Newtonian concepts at that time. The malleability of time and space follows from the fact that speed – any speed – is measured by dividing distance (space) by duration (time). This is the definition of speed: a certain distance traveled in a certain amount of time. In other words, we measure the speed of light by saying it has traveled x miles in y seconds. When we do measure it we get the whopping speed of 186,000 miles per second (or 300,000 kilometers per second).

The strange nature of relativity theory is made evident when we consider two observers looking at the same phenomenon. Imagine you are a scientist on Earth and you measure the time it takes for light to reach us from the Sun. If we already know the speed of light and we know the distance of the Sun from Earth, we can easily calculate the time it takes to reach us. You, as a scientist, conclude correctly that it takes about eight minutes.

Imagine now a second observer, an alien whizzing past our solar system at a constant velocity of half the speed of light. To the alien, the speed of light from the Sun to Earth is the same: it's still 186,000 miles per second. Remember that this is the basic assumption in special relativity: the speed of light remains the same no matter how fast the observer is traveling. But if the speed is constant for both you on Earth and the alien traveling at half the speed of light, then space and time cannot be constant. They must, instead, be malleable. So for the alien observing light traveling from Sun to Earth, the distance from Sun to Earth will be different from what you on Earth measure it to be, and the time it takes for the light to travel will be different. In fact, when we apply the equations of special relativity to this example, the space alien will conclude, from its vantage point, that the distance between Sun and Earth is almost one-sixth shorter than you on Earth conclude that it is. And the alien will conclude that the time it takes for light to travel from Sun to Earth is almost one-sixth less than it appears to take from your point of view on Earth. Space and time become malleable.

This, then, is the basis for Einstein's assertion that there is no absolute time and no absolute space. It's all relative. There is no universal now, so determining whether one event, for example, an electrical short in the alien's dashboard, is simultaneous with the sun rising at a certain place on Earth, is *relative*. This means that for different observers examining these two events, different conclusions about their simultaneity, or lack thereof, may be validly offered. This is known as the "relativity of simultaneity." If simultaneity is relative, there is no real distinction between past, present and future: the apparent distinction is just a stubbornly persistent illusion based on our Earth-bound biological heritage that lacks experience with these kinds of things.

But is this how the universe really works? Or is relativity theory just one useful way of looking at these concepts that may not reflect the more fundamental reality? We discussed in earlier chapters how indeed our evolved senses can at times mislead us because we have evolved ways to perceive only the aspects of our world that were more or less necessary for the survival and propagation of our species and our forebears. But this doesn't mean that all common sense views about the nature of reality are illusory. The deep nature of time, it so happens, does in fact mesh quite well with our common sense views of time when we bushwhack our way through the confusion of today's physical theories.

The idea that time is an illusion, the prevailing view among physicists and philosophers in the beginning of the 21st Century, also forces the conclusion that free will is an illusion and that we live in a deterministic universe. Einstein himself struggled mightily with his deterministic view of the universe, the idea that time is illusory, and the impacts of these notions on human free will. He never found a fully satisfactory resolution.

I believe, along with a growing number of philosophers and physicists, that there are other ways of explaining the universe that don't lead to the conclusion that time is an illusion. A promising alternative to Einstein's theories was developed initially by Hendrik Lorentz, the Dutch Nobel Prize-winning physicist we've encountered previously, a few years before Einstein developed his own theories. Lorentz developed the mathematics that Einstein used in his own theory of special relativity (known as the "Lorentz transformations"), but Lorentz interpreted the mathematics quite differently. And Lorentz did not postulate that the speed of light was constant for all observers. Rather, Lorentz thought that an immaterial ether (this is different than the earlier idea of the "luminiferous ether") was the medium through which light traveled. For Lorentz, the ether had avoided detection, in experiments like the famous Michelson-Morley experiment of 1887, in which the speed of light in relation to the Earth was found to be constant despite the Earth's rotation around the Sun, because matter contracts as its speed increases. It contracts based on the dragging effect the ether has on all matter, similar to how matter contracts or expands when it is, respectively, cooled or heated. If matter contracts based on its interaction with the ether, at high speeds relative to the ether (Lorentz), we obtain the same experimental results as if we assume that the speed of light is constant for all observers (Einstein). So these two approaches are different interpretations, not fundamentally different theories.

Today, for those who have considered the competing interpretations of Einstein and Lorentz, the general conclusion is that they are empirically indistinguishable. The large majority of physicists and philosophers conclude, however, that Einstein's approach is better for other reasons. I disagree on this point but we needn't go into details here other than to note that there are legitimate alternatives to Einstein's theories and that the alleged illusory nature of time is, thus, not a *necessary* conclusion. Lorentzian relativity seems to be making a comeback in the early part of the 21st Century, with a number of "dissident" physicists highlighting this alternative theory and other alternatives to Einstein's theories.

A key feature of reality that Einstein and many other thinkers seem to have overlooked is that, despite the fact that we may, as an abstract exercise, consider time to be like another spatial dimension, time is not in actuality like the traditional spatial dimensions. Time is not a dimension. Rather, time is, as a one-way and ongoing laying down of the universe, simply change from one state of the universe to the next. Time is thus fundamental and inescapable. Time is asymmetrical and spatial dimensions are symmetrical. And consciousness is integrally connected to time. Consciousness and time are twin aspects of a single process, the creative advance, which is the process by which the universe comes into being in each moment, as it emanates from the ground of being/ether. More generally, the relativistic view that time is malleable leads to self-contradiction and to contradictions of our deeply held intuitions about the nature of time and free will. If we can resolve these self-contradictions and more general contradictions with a different view of time and free will, while adhering to the scientific method, shouldn't such an alternative be very seriously considered?

There are many asserted self-contradictions – paradoxes – that stem from Einstein's relativity theories. I will consider only one here. According to relativity theory, there is no distinction between past, present and future. Time's arrow works equally well in either direction, according to various prevailing theories (not just relativity theory). We can, under the equations of general relativity, in principle travel back in time, even if we don't actually know how to do it at this point in our scientific knowledge. However, if time travel to the past is possible, what happens if a time-traveling woman killed her own mother, through accident or design, before the time traveler herself was born? Does she suddenly disappear because she's "changed" the past? Or does the universe conspire to somehow prevent her from ever completing such a paradoxical act? Both of these options are highly problematic for many reasons. This paradox is in fact the subject of much philosophical debate and science fiction speculation. It highlights just one of the many difficulties that arise from considering time capable of proceeding backwards as well as forwards, or of time travel into the past.

Thinking about the nature of time is inherently difficult because of time's universality. Ask a fish what water is and, if the fish could actually ponder such a question and reply, it would probably say "what on Earth do you mean?" Just as water is the ever-present, and thus un-noticed, container for our smart fish and her entire universe, time is the ever-present container for our entire existence. To exist, to be, is to be in time. More technically: existence requires temporal existence. Explaining the most common features of our existence is perhaps the most difficult task of philosophy and science because there are no analogies to compare to time – time is unique. As in earlier chapters, the process philosophy of Alfred North Whitehead and his intellectual heirs provides a framework to aid our understanding.

As mentioned, time is, at its root, simply change. We know change is real by simply looking around: everywhere we look there is change. The ability to look around itself is change: changing contents of our consciousness, changing positions of our head, neck and eyeballs, etc., in each moment. Support for this view of time as just change may be found in current definitions of time as a unit of measurement – the International Standard (SI) unit of time is now defined by an exact number of oscillations in a cesium atom (9,192,631,770 transitions between two different states). In other words, the basic unit of time is now defined by a precise number of measurable changes in a specific physical system.

The prevailing – and highly counter-intuitive – view, however, among scientists and philosophers is that the appearance of change is in fact illusory. These scholars argue that things *seem* to change, from our human perspective, but that this change is not fundamental. The universe's entire past, present and future are, in reality, already in existence "in block." Whatever we consider "now," from our particular vantage point, is simply one of an infinite number of moments, or slices, in the infinite block universe that already exists. Time is in this view more about location than about time as a progression of moments.

But if this is the case, how do we explain the *appearance* of change, our subjective experience of time? This is an entirely unresolved issue in modern physics. As I've suggested already, we have two ways of proceeding: we either reinterpret Einstein's relativity theories or we take a different approach entirely. Either way, there is some feature of our universe that needs explanation: the apparent one-way passage of time. As with the concept of "matter," it doesn't really matter (all puns intended) what we call these concepts. What does matter, if we are seeking a rigorous basis for science and/or spirituality, is that we explain these features of our reality, regardless of what we call them. In sum, the appearance of change must be explained, either as something that is ultimately illusory, and how that view meshes with the overwhelming evidence of our senses; or something that is in fact a real, fundamental, feature of the universe. And the modern view that sees the passage of time as an illusion has not done either.

David Ray Griffin, an American philosopher who is one of Whitehead's most prominent intellectual heirs, points out that there are three key aspects to time "as we experience it": 1) asymmetry; 2) constant becoming; and 3) irreversibility. *Asymmetry* refers to the fact that time does not operate the same backwards and forwards. To the contrary, we remember the past and look forward to the future. Our linguistic conventions reflect the fundamental differences between past and future. We live in the present and only in the present. This asymmetry is also present, as we know from experiment, even at the most fundamental physical level of atoms and subatomic particles. (One of the key problems in modern physics, as mentioned, is that our current physical theories do not reflect this observed asymmetry). We cannot actually stop time, despite our ability to conceptually "freeze" a moment – and this feature of reality is what Griffin refers to as *constant becoming*. Time is, time passes, never stopping. *Irreversibility* refers to the fact that not only can we not stop time, we also can't reverse its direction. Time has an arrow and it points in only one direction: straight ahead to the future.

Griffin distinguishes "soft-core" common sense from "hard-core" common sense. Soft-core common sense is, for example, the idea that of course the world is flat. We can just look out and see that it's flat. This is only soft-core common sense, however, because the world is of course not flat. It is, in fact, undeniable that the world is a sphere, based on abundant and incontrovertible evidence. Science has knocked down many of our soft-core common sense notions.

It is commonly supposed that the appearance of change, of time, has also been knocked down by modern science. Time's forward flow, and its other key features described by Griffin, are, however, an example of hard-core common sense. We cannot contradict hard-core common sense without at the same time contradicting ourselves in the very same act. A philosopher may state that time is illusory but the very act of making this statement involves duration – change. There was a moment before the philosopher issued her statement. There was a moment in which she issued the statement. And there is a moment after she issued her statement. There was, in a word, change, or at least the appearance of change. In either alternative, there is something – objective time or subjective time – that needs explaining.

Free will is another example of Griffin's hard-core common sense. A philosopher cannot choose to deny free will without contradicting the assertion by this very act. This is known as "performative contradiction."

One alternative to relativity theory, and the absolute speed of light that forms its core, is taking the passage of time to be absolute instead. Absolute time was made explicit by Newton in his most famous work, *Principia Mathematica*, a set of theories that prevailed for over two hundred years as the dominant theory of gravity, space and time. However, the concept of absolute time was generally abandoned by physicists once Einstein's theories became widely adopted in the first half of the 20th Century, in favor of the concepts of relative simultaneity and relative time. As we have seen in earlier chapters, there is a new push in the last few decades favoring alternatives to relativity theory, such as Lorentz's ether theory. Lorentz's theory supports the concept of absolute time, as well as absolute motion, instead of the malleable notion of time contained in Einstein's relativity theory.

The concept of absolute time or "real time" is, in my view, the better story about time. Smolin's 2013 book, *Time Reborn,* fleshes out many physical theories and ideas in an extended argument for real time, as opposed to the "time is illusory" school of thought. My favoring of real time follows, in particular, from the quantum non-locality (entanglement) experiments discussed in previous chapters and our experience of time as a progress of moments (a "flow"). The non-locality experiments established the reality of non-locality, or, at the least, the possibility of signals traveling at speeds far faster than the speed of light rather than instantaneously. If this is the case, Einstein's basic postulate of the constancy of the speed of light, and the conclusion that the speed of light as an ultimate speed limit for our universe, are undermined. We are, then, led to contemplate anew alternatives to Einstein's theories, including Lorentz's ether theory as one of the more promising alternatives. With Lorentz's theory, there is no "block universe," in which past, present and future all exist at the same time. There is no relativity of simultaneity. Thus the *apparent* flow of time, which is undeniable, is meshed with an *actual* flow of time in the objective universe. The full story is, of course, far more complex than I have outlined here, but this discussion conveys the essentials.

In this view of time, we may envision reality – to simplify reality into a more graspable *model* of reality – as a pristine sandy beach. The wave front, constantly crashing onto shore and then receding, and then crashing again, represents the ongoing creation of reality. The wave front is the present. The wide ocean behind the wave front is the past, guiding the wave front. The oscillation between receding wave front and crashing wave front represents the oscillation between subject and object in each part of the universe. The progression of time is the result of each new wave crashing onto the shore, a result of the ocean behind it and all previous waves. The degree to which this process is deterministic or a result of free will requires transcending this limited model and is the subject of the next chapter.

The idea that physics shows time to be ultimately unreal would put physics ... in contradiction with our hard-core convictions about freedom, creativity, and moral values .... The truth, however, is that physics itself does not entail the unreality of time. That interpretation results only from a materialistic view of the entities studied by physics....

21st Century American philosopher David Ray Griffin (2007)

Chapter 17: Free will goes all the way down

The concept of time described here has another very helpful consequence: it preserves free will. Einstein never resolved his own intuitions about free will and the nature of time. He was forced under his own theories to conclude that he himself lacked free will because all beings lack free will if time is illusory. If the past, present and future *already exist*, then how can any action I "choose" now have an impact on the already existing future? It can't. This was for Einstein a difficult but necessary conclusion that resulted from his theories about time and the nature of the universe more generally.

This difficulty should not be surprising because most people find this to be a difficult conclusion. It contradicts our common-sense notion of our ability to make real choices. Free will is at the root of our society in many ways, including in law, morality, religion, relationships, and practically every aspect of human activity. Fortunately, believing that free will is an illusion is not in fact a necessary conclusion of modern physics or neuroscience. The concept of time I've already described preserves free will and results in a universe that is infinitely creative and non-deterministic. In this universe, free will exists at all levels of reality and we are each of us unfettered in creating our preferred future. Not only are humans infinitely creative and free to do as we wish, the *entire universe and every constituent of the universe* is also unfettered at the most basic level. We are led to this conclusion by considering the nature of matter and the ether/ground of being, as we have done in previous chapters. Whitehead stated that the "laws of nature are more accurately described as the habits of nature." Habits are a function of choice, of free will, and may be broken. The habits of nature obviously lead to regularity and predictability in most ways – if they didn't, they couldn't be called habits and none of our technologies would work in a reliable way. But the habits of nature never act as an absolute limit on creativity and freedom. Habits don't do anything. Habits are just a label for observed behaviors. Just as we can deviate from our ingrained habits when we choose to, so nature and every constituent of nature can deviate from habit.

Interestingly, if we view time as an illusion we are led to a radical reduction in freedom. This is the case because even if we conceptually break loose from the chains on viewing time as necessarily unidirectional and omnipresent, as Einstein and countless others have done in the last century, we shackle ourselves with heavier chains by doing so. Free will cannot exist in a universe where past, present and future exist already, in "block." The alternative, which I advocate, is that if we see time as unidirectional and omnipresent, as part of the creative advance that perpetually re-creates the universe in each moment, human freedom is assured. The universe is wide open as we look forward, we are active players in creating our own future, and the entire universe – not just human beings – becomes imbued with innate freedom and creativity.

There are many routes to this conclusion. One path to free will can be traveled in just two simple steps: 1) we never know the full extent of what we don't know – including all relevant laws of physics; 2) thus, we don't know the full extent of the influences on any particular decision we make, so we can simply choose to believe we have free will with respect to our choices. It really can be as simple as this. This argument is as powerful as it is simple.

Going a little deeper, however, and fleshing out some of Whitehead's ideas on the nature of matter, time and free will, let's examine what Whitehead called events. This examination is a key step in making our case for the existence of free will at all levels of reality. events, as discussed, are the fundamental constituents of matter, experience and time. Each event is a "drop of experience" because, for Whitehead, what we call matter cannot be devoid of experience or consciousness. Taking consciousness seriously, as we must if we are being rational, we must also realize that for consciousness to exist at all in a world comprised of matter, the potentiality of human consciousness must be present in all matter, when arranged in the right kind of configuration. If it wasn't, we couldn't be here. We are here; ergo, matter must contain the seeds of human-level consciousness from the very beginning. So every event has two basic aspects:

an objective aspect, which we traditionally call matter, and a subjective aspect, which we call experience, consciousness or mind, depending on the level of complexity present. For Whitehead, these two aspects oscillate back and forth in an ongoing process from subject to object to subject to object... Each event, when it is a subject, takes all the information available to it and *decides* how to manifest objectively. This process applies to all things, from an electron, to a gnat, a bat, a rat, a cat, a human, and probably to higher levels of consciousness. Thus, free will – the choice of how to manifest objectively – is built into fundamental reality. It is highly rudimentary in most event because most events (electrons, protons, atoms, etc.) are highly rudimentary and their consciousness is equally rudimentary. But this consciousness and associated free will complexifies and evolves as matter complexifies and evolves, particularly in living things.

This approach is reminiscent of the discussion in Chapter 2 on consciousness as the bridge between matter and spirit. I showed how consciousness can be broken down into three conceptual parts: subject, object, and a link between the two. Each event, as described in this chapter, starts as a subject, perceives all possible objects around it through the various linkages offered by the physical forces of electromagnetism, gravity, etc. and then chooses how to manifest objectively. When this happens, the subject becomes an object and is now available to be perceived by all other subjects in the next moment. And so on.

In a little less abstract representation, this is the foamy wave front described in the previous chapter. Every subject throughout the vast extent of the universe goes through this same process and represents a tiny speck of foam in that infinite wave as it crashes onto the shore. Thus, every aspect of that vast wave chooses how to manifest and makes its mark on the shore. Then it recedes back into subjectivity as the wave pulls back and prepares for the next moment.

The word will, which, like a magic spell, is to reveal to us the essence of everything in nature, by no means designates an unknown quantity, something arrived at only by inference, but rather something that is in every way immediately recognized and so familiar to us that we know and understand what will is far better than anything else. The concept of will has hitherto commonly been subordinated to that of force, but I do the very opposite, and desire that every force in nature should be thought of as will.

Arthur Schopenhauer, The World as Will and Idea (1819)

Part IV: The nature of the Self

You are the universe. You are God. You are Brahman. You are the ocean of being. You are the All. Yet you don't always feel like this is true! In fact, most of us never enjoy the experience of full *gnosis*, of God-realization. There certainly is *some* distinction between me, as a small human being, and the rest of the infinitely large universe around me. And even if this isn't the ultimate deeper reality, how do we explain the *apparent* distinction in our perceived reality? What is this "self" that seems to be *in here*, as opposed to the rest of the universe *out there*? And how does it relate to the true Self, Source, Brahman, the All?

Chapter 18: You are not who you think you are

I've already spoiled many times over any surprise regarding the key theme of this book: you are not who you think you are. You are not merely a little bag of flesh and bones living a short pointless existence on a small planet in a backwater galaxy in a cold and unfriendly universe. Nor are you an eternal and unchanging soul subject to the dictates of a distant and unknowable patriarchal God, who may reward or punish you based on seemingly arbitrary, outdated and sometimes cruel or nonsensical rules. You are neither of these extremes of human thought. You are, instead, the entire universe, the wave and the ocean at the same time. You are God. You are Brahman, you are Source, and a little bag of flesh and bones too. You are all of it.

Why isn't this truth more widespread? Why isn't it "normal" to make such claims, instead of being literally heretical in many religious traditions and inscrutable under the gaze of conventional materialism? I can't answer such questions here and they are anyway unanswerable in principle. A large part of making these truths better understood and more widespread requires that we better understand the "self," the topic of this chapter. In this discussion, we must re-visit our conclusions regarding consciousness and experience.

Experience is the more fundamental feature of what we commonly refer to as consciousness. Experience is innate in all matter and, when matter combines in certain complex ways and creates a model of the world in order to navigate that world, such as in human brains and in many other animals, and *includes a model of itself* in that model of the world, a complex "self" arises.

What is this self, at the individual human level of existence? In other words, what is the nature of individual identity and our normal sense of self? Experience is that undeniable feature of reality that we all can confirm in any given moment with the Cartesian realization: "I think, therefore I am." In this story, this statement becomes, however: "I experience, therefore *experience exists*." The distinction between experience and the *self*, the "I," hinges on the fact that a self requires a longer duration to exist than a pure moment of experience. Each self is the connection of moments of experience into a stream of experience/consciousness. Experience may be considered instantaneous: it exists in this moment, and now this one, and now this one... It's not *really* instantaneous because every experience must have some duration, albeit small. But the self is generally conceived as possessing some degree of continuity – this is what it means to have a self: relative continuity. In other words, the distinction between self and experience is that self is experience extending over many moments with some continuity between each moment. But what is "self" beyond this distinction, and is this a real difference?

I will offer a quick clarification at this point: this difference between "self" and "experience" is not particularly important. Rather, experience is the more fundamental feature of our universe, and self is an abstraction we place on top of experience. This abstraction is not unimportant because there is an obvious continuity between moments of experience for each of us, but it's not really a difference in kind from the pure experience of each moment. Experience may be considered singular and the self may be considered simply the plural of experience—a collection of related experiences over time.

In common parlance, however, the self is the sum total of who we are as individuals. My "self" is the essence of who I am. Most of us would agree that we do change as human beings, and thus that our "selves" change. But the vast majority of people still imagine some permanence to the self, consciously or unconsciously. In the religious and spiritual context, this sense of permanence is called the soul. This is a highly important concept in almost all spiritual traditions. But is there a soul, is there an essence that represents who we really are?

In answering these questions we run yet again into problems with the nature of words as limited tools. The soul is a concept that would seem to have a necessary place in any comprehensive spirituality. This is not, however, necessarily the case. As just mentioned, *experience* (consciousness) is the more fundamental feature that we are trying to explain when we use terms like "soul." There is no particular harm, however, in thinking of ourselves as having souls, as long as we recognize that there is nothing permanent about a soul. The common concept of the soul can be misleading if we view the soul as the *unchanging* essence of who each of us is, and something that is fundamentally separate from our bodies and brains. There is, however, nothing unchanging in this universe, including "souls." The soul, by tradition, is thought to be our true, eternal, nature. And in some traditions, the soul travels between bodies and perhaps between the earthly realm and other realms. Most damaging, however, is the notion of the self as the subject of eternal damnation if certain dictates are crossed. We can't read the Old Testament without gaining a clear sense of an angry and jealous God who will subject individual souls to all manner of eternal hell-fire with minimal justification.

Thankfully, however, change and impermanence are inescapable features of the universe. Similarly, the closer we examine the idea of the soul, the more clear it becomes that the notion of an enduring self, either in the secular sense, or in the more religious sense of the soul, is truly an illusion because change is inescapable. This is a difficult idea for many to accept. And I recognize fully that whether one chooses to believe in an unchanging soul, or not, is a highly personal decision. The flip-side of eternal damnation is eternal bliss and this is the promised reward in many traditions for those who observe God's dictates. This is in many ways a highly appealing notion. For me, however, it seems clear that the common view of one's soul as unchanging essence is both an unnecessary concept and one that is hard to justify rationally. I can't rule it out, of course, because I can never know the full extent of what I don't know. The existence of an unchanging soul in each of us nevertheless seems quite unlikely. This is one of the basic teachings of Buddhism, and some other religious and spiritual traditions. It is a truth originally derived without the aid of modern science and its knowledge of atoms, molecules and metabolism. Modern physics, chemistry and biology have done much, however, to bolster the ancient teachings in this area.

In Buddhism, this idea is known as "no-self" or *anatman*. The *atman* is the Hindu version of what we call in the West the soul. The key difference between the Hindu tradition and the Judeo-Christian tradition is that the atman is ultimately the same as Brahman. Atman is a drop of Brahman in each of us. In the Western tradition, we can, through right belief and right action, attain the Kingdom of God and sit in the same realm as God. But we are not the same as God and never will be. To consider ourselves ultimately the same as God has been considered heresy, in the Christian tradition, for millennia. Part VI delves into these ideas further.

Buddha contradicted the Hindu tradition of his day, which he grew up with in 5th Century BCE India. As with Jesus growing up in the Judaic tradition, Buddha was raised in an ancient tradition and eventually found good reasons to contradict many key teachings of the ancient tradition he was raised in. Buddha, contrary to the Hindu teachings, could find no reason to believe in atman, the permanent self. To the Buddha, all things are ultimately empty of any inherent nature. All things are relational – they arise through "dependent origination," to use the common English translation of this doctrine. In Western terms, Buddha denied the reality of the soul. This is the *anatman* doctrine.

Was Buddha right, and does it really matter? Buddha, in his original teachings, avoided discussions of metaphysics because he thought such discussions were unfruitful and not helpful for the true goal of spirituality: liberation from the self. Later schools of Buddhist thought failed to heed Buddha's example and many different schools have since developed detailed metaphysical views. Buddha didn't have much to say about Brahman, but he did talk about "emptiness." As with the "vacuum" of modern physics, however, Buddha's emptiness, now part of many Buddhist schools of thought, is not really empty. It is, in fact, everything. Emptiness is not nothing, it's no thing. That is, there are no things, only processes, only change—just as in contemporary process philosophy in the Western tradition.

So for Buddha even though all things are ultimately relational with respect to their existence, he advocated a concept, which he called emptiness, which performs the same conceptual role as Brahman performs in Hinduism. Do Buddhism and Hinduism still disagree on this issue? If you asked ten Buddhists and ten Hindus this question, you would probably receive twenty different answers. I believe, however, that Buddha's emptiness is equivalent in many ways to Brahman, particularly if we accept that Brahman, Source, etc., is always changing. Where Buddha's real difference with Hinduism lies is his denial of the reality of the atman, the soul. And here is where I think Buddha's departure from Hinduism is helpful and valid.

Regardless of terminology, or of the reality or unreality of a permanent self or soul, it seems clear that we may arrive at the same endpoint, the *gnosis/Samadhi/satori* experience, by realizing the nature of our own experience as part of the same seamless fabric of *maya,* the physical universe, and ultimately our oneness with Brahman/Source. It's all just one thing and we are it. Brahman is the ultimate Self. In this manner, there is a ground of sorts available to us. If we need a safe harbor, Brahman is it.

But as discussed previously, even Brahman, our Source, changes over time. We know with certainty that its emanations – the universe of *maya* – are always changing. We are part of the seamless whole that is the universe, thus we are it. We don't know, and will never know, whether Brahman itself is a permanent reality or if it had some beginning and even perhaps an end. We do know, however, that all else is in perpetual flux and all features of our universe more generally melt into dust in the course of time.

My view is that Source is eternal but always changing. The physical universe that emanates from Source is most likely cyclical, with island universes coming into being and eventually dissipating through the infinite expanse of space through infinite eons. We are at the beginning of our current cycle in our own island universe and we have an exciting few trillion years ahead of us as the ascent of consciousness continues and we help to spread consciousness and spirit throughout the universe as we learn how to leave our beautiful spherical home and thrive on other planets and, before too long, other star systems.

Chapter 19: The little self is always changing and shouldn't be taken too seriously

If Brahman is the only real Self, how do we deal with the personal self, the "little self," in each of us? There is a sense in which the little self is very real. Our little self is the socially constructed self. Our socially constructed selves define us, exalt us, and sometimes restrict us. We even think sometimes of our little selves in the third person. "Tam Hunt" is a lawyer, scholar, and writer who lives in Santa Barbara. "Tam Hunt" is 45 years old. "Tam Hunt" plays a lot of tennis and has a pretty good serve on a good day. "Tam Hunt" has a number of friends and acquaintances, some of whom appreciate him more than others, some of whom are more reliable than others, etc. The little self is commonly described as the ego.

By being human we create a little self, a socially constructed self. This self doesn't exist when we are born and it gradually comes into being as our parents, siblings and associates co-create, with our budding sense of the universe around us, our little self. And this is the point of the little self: it is indeed entirely relational, as Buddha pointed out. Everything about us, which we consider to be who we are as individuals, depends on the values and judgments of others. By necessity, then, our happiness or lack thereof also depends on the values and judgments of others. Buddha was thus entirely right about "no-self" as it concerns the little self.

As we've seen, fortunately, the little self is not *really* who we are. It's not anything permanent at all. Everything about the little self can and does change, including body and mind. Names seem to have some degree of permanence, but they can just as well change. And hanging our true nature on a name seems to be a bit precarious and lacking in real depth.

Despite the illusory nature of the little self, it is undeniably important to the vast majority of us as imperfect human beings. So what do we do with this pesky thing, the little self? The Hindu tradition of the stages of life is a useful framework, particularly when we overlay it with some of Buddha's insights. Many of Christ's admonitions about the good life are completely congruent with the Buddhist and Hindu traditions and are also very helpful.

The Hindu stages of life consist of a very general guide for living. Each of us should be a student early in life, a householder to raise a family, a contemplative upon retirement, and finally a wanderer who renounces the physical and social worlds during old age. I reduce these stages to three and attempt to soften the edges a bit of what can seem to modern ears fairly harsh prescriptions for right living.

Being a student is self-explanatory. We learn how to be in the world, how to understand the world, how to relate to others, how to have a career, etc. This stage has over human history become longer and longer as human culture has become more complex. It is not uncommon now for people to be students into their early thirties. This is not a bad thing because the life of the mind, of being a student eager to learn, should in fact continue in some manner throughout every stage of life. Writing a book is a great way to gain new understandings…

Becoming a householder is also self-explanatory. As biological beings with a natural desire to have offspring and to share our history with the next generation, we need to find the stability to find a mate and to raise a family. This does not mean, however, that we ignore the spiritual quest during this stage. Rather, we should pursue our livelihoods and our relationships in a way that helps us to grow, understand, and to progress toward our true Self. Buddha's "right livelihood" urges us to choose careers that don't conflict with the ultimate goal of life: awakening, God-realization. Paramahansa Yogananda, an Indian sage who devoted his life to spreading India's philosophy in the Western world during the 20th Century, advised: "Everything else can wait, but your search for God cannot wait."

Last, we retire from the householder role and resume our student life, but in a far more substantial way. We have gained the experience of our earlier student life as well as our householder years. We have gained much wisdom. In our retirement, we apply this wisdom to attain the *lived* understanding of our true Self. The traditional Hindu way was to become a *sanyassin*, a traveling beggar with nothing but a bowl to his or her name. This was in fact a widely practiced tradition at various stages in Indian culture. It is not, however, practical in the western world in the early part of the 21st Century for retirees to renounce all things and wander with nothing but a begging bowl.

Yet there is an undeniable poetry and good sense to this framework. It helps us integrate the little self with its various parts and, more importantly, the true Self becomes apparent. We live our lives in such a way that we acknowledge our biological imperatives – or at least our strong biological prods – by having a family; we acknowledge our socially constructed roles by building a career and contributing to our communities and societies; and we acknowledge the need to eventually realize our true Self by returning to pure contemplation once our biological and social roles are satisfied.

We gain a large headstart, however, in attaining an early understanding of who we really are. With this understanding, an early God-realization, we may navigate more gracefully through life, surfing the waves of fortune and misfortune with equanimity and relish. We see the little self as a social construct and thus don't take it too seriously. We can observe it and we can laugh at it. We should always laugh at it.

Chapter 20: Kill your little self because the true Self never dies

Death is viewed with dread by most cultures, including our own. It kept me awake at night when I was a child – along with countless other children (and adults) throughout history. To my childhood self, the thought of my nonexistence was too terrible to bear and I attempted not to think about it as much as possible. This, as one may imagine, led to the opposite result and I did spend a fair amount of time as a youngster thinking about the fate that we are all destined to follow – and I still do now as an adult as the signs of age begin to manifest more strongly. Even more alarming to my young self was the idea that my parents would eventually die, and that we would *all* eventually die. I imagined death as a downward spiral in empty space, eventually resulting in … nothingness. This and similar visions are surely the basis for many cultures' notions of life after death, in which those who lead good lives are rewarded in some fashion by a new and better life after leaving this world and a far worse fate for those who did not lead good lives.

The Buddhist response to fear of death and other sources of suffering is to realize the truth of "no-self," to realize that it's all a web of inter-related emptiness, including our concept of self. The Hindu Vedanta response is even deeper: by recognizing our true Self, Brahman, ocean of being, the All, etc., we realize that infinitely larger Self that never dies. This knowledge allows us to accept with greater equanimity and grace the inevitable decline and eventual dissolution of the little self, back into that deep ocean, as our body dissolves with death.

While the little self has enabled us to climb the highest mountains – literally and figuratively – and to achieve countless other great things, the little self is also the bane of our existence. It's never happy – at least not for very long. It's always directing our body to do this and do that, from the moment we wake to the moment we return to sleep. Go go go. It also gets sick, grows old and dies, and worries about these things before they happen. What if we could just turn the little self off for a while? What would happen then? What if we could temporarily kill the little self? What if we could permanently kill the little self?

Killing the little self is the point of Buddhism, Hindu Vedanta, and many other spiritual practices, even if this exact terminology is not used. Killing the self is yet another term for *gnosis*, the knowledge of our true Self, God-realization. By killing the little self, we travel through life more gracefully, more fully in the moment, secure in our knowledge that we are the true Self, we are Brahman. When we loosen the grip of the tyrannical little self, the joyous experience inherent just beneath the surface, pure bliss, becomes manifest. Achieving this level of *lived* understanding is the objective of our time here now.

With this new/old understanding of the impermanence of the little self, we see that at the point of bodily death "I" don't die because I am/you are always the totality, the All, the ocean. What dies is simply the conventional view of selfhood, the little self – highly important from a practical, everyday point of view, but not our deeper self. I, with the death of my body, continue on as my true Self. The true Self has always existed and will always exist. From Brahman's point of view, my larger Self's point of view, the death of the little self is akin to a leaf falling from a tree or a wave disappearing from the surface of the ocean. The tree itself remains strong and the ocean doesn't notice. We realize also that we are not really that leaf or that little wave. We are the tree, the mightiest oak that ever lived; we are the ocean, we are all of the oceans on every planet in every universe. We are all of it.

Words and concepts split life into separate segments that have no reality in themselves. We could even say that the notion "my life" is the original delusion of separateness, the source of ego. If I and life are two, if I am separate from life, then I am separate from all things, all beings, all people. But how could I be separate from life? What "I" could there be apart from life, apart from Being? It is utterly impossible. So there is no such thing as "my life," and I don't have a life. I am life. I and life are one. It cannot be otherwise. So how could I lose my life? How can I lose something that I don't have in the first place? How can I lose something that I Am? It is impossible.

21ˢᵗ Century German author Eckhart Tolle,
A New Earth (2005)

When I stand by the stream and watch it, I am relatively still, and the flowing water makes a path across my memory so that I realize its transience in comparison with my stability. This is, of course, an illusion in the sense that I too am in flow and likewise have no final destination .... My death will be the disappearance of a particular pattern in the water.

20ᵗʰ Century British philosopher Alan Watts, *Cloud Hidden, Whereabouts Unknown* (1971)

Part V: The nature of life

A major advance in our understanding of the universe and of ourselves since the Buddha's time and since the time of Christ occurred with the advent of modern biology. This knowledge is very helpful for achieving the lasting integration of our various selves, which includes our biological selves. We've been discussing life – biological life – as though we know what it is, but we'll see in the following chapters that this seemingly obvious concept is actually rather problematic. To understand what it means to be an embodied biological organism, we need to understand what "life" is. We know that we are alive. And we know that whales and trees, for example, are also alive. But what are the defining features, if any, of life? And why does this matter? How does biology connect with consciousness and with spirituality?

There is grandeur in this view of life.... From so simple a beginning, endless forms most beautiful and most wonderful have been, and are being evolved.

Charles Darwin, *On the Origin of Species* (1859)

In a way, nature is alive ... all the way to the depths.

20th Century American physicist David Bohm (1982)

Chapter 21: Life, like consciousness, goes all the way down

What is life? Is life something that, like obscenity, we "know it when we see it?" If only it were that easy. Unfortunately, every definition of life provided thus far runs into serious problems. Sole and Goodwin (2000) say it well: "Grasping the nature of life is like catching a whirling eddy in a stream: the moment you have it in your hands it disappears and leaves you with the matter but not the form." But Aristotle perhaps said it best: "Nothing is true of that which is changing." We may carve out generally workable definitions, as rules of thumb (*heuristics*) for deeper study, but we must always acknowledge that any definition regarding physical phenomena that ignores the truth of flux fails from the outset.

Numerous modern biologists have attempted to answer the question: what is life? J.B.S. Haldane, the 20th Century British biologist considered to be a giant in his field, began a short essay, entitled "What is Life"? by stating: "I am not going to answer this question." There are also three books from the 20th Century alone, with the same title, which attempt to answer this eons-old question. Erwin Schrödinger, a paragon of modern physics well-known for his role in shaping quantum theory, described in his little 1935 masterpiece, *What is Life?*, the concept of negative entropy, or *negentropy*, as the defining characteristic of life. Contrary to the Second Law of Thermodynamics, which asserts that the general tendency in our universe is for order to decay into disorder – entropy – the tendency of life, indeed the very defining characteristic of life, is the opposite. Schrödinger defines life by its ability to create order out of disorder, to defy the trends that inanimate matter must otherwise follow. This definition is intriguing, but more recent knowledge about the self-organizing characteristics of what is normally considered inanimate matter renders it problematic as a definition of life as something distinct and qualitatively different from non-living matter. When water freezes it transitions from a less ordered state to a more ordered state. This is negentropy. But is water alive? I don't think Schrödinger would have said so. What about crystals more generally, whether of water, silicon or metal? Indeed, we shall see below that there isn't really any clear separation from what is negentropic and what is not. If life is defined as what is negentropic, then the whole universe is in some manner negentropic because key parts of the universe are negentropic. Hold that thought.

Ernst Mayr, an American, was another giant of biology in the 20th Century. He taught at Harvard for decades and, after he had retired, wrote his encyclopedic overview of biology, *The Growth of Biological Thought*, and many other books. He acknowledged the difficulty in defining life: "Attempts have been made again and again to define 'life.' These endeavors are rather futile since it is now clear that there is no special substance, object, or force that can be identified with life."

Mayr couldn't resist however, proposing his own list of criteria to describe the "process of living," as opposed to "life." Mayr's criteria for living processes were:

- complexity and organization
- chemical uniqueness
- quality
- uniqueness and variability
- a genetic program
- a historical nature
- natural selection
- indeterminacy.

I won't go into details regarding Mayr's system except to say that Mayr, despite his own cautions, falls right into the same trap he warned about with his criteria for living processes that he warned about in refusing to define "life." All of Mayr's criteria either fall on a continuum or are arbitrary distinctions proposed intuitively and without a deeper foundational principle. Why must life have a genetic program, and what does this even mean? Does the genetic program have to be DNA? Can it be bits of code in a computer? Mayr's writings on these questions reveals his own lack of resolve on this topic. He suggests that computers and software may contain instructions akin to DNA, but then fails to explain why software "DNA" is qualitatively different than non-software DNA. The same can be said with respect to all of his criteria.

A simpler definition of life is offered by American biologist Benton Clark. He reduces the criteria for life to just three:

- Reproduction
- Using energy
- Containing instructions in the organism

Clark, realizing that mules or humans who choose not to reproduce would not be considered alive under this definition, distinguishes "life forms" from "organisms." The latter category includes mules and non-reproducing humans. Life forms are comprised of individual organisms and must reproduce to be considered alive under Clark's definitions.

Clark's definition of life forms gives rise to the possibility that mechanical or electronic creatures may be considered to be alive, assuming such creatures will eventually be able to reproduce themselves, as they surely will in coming years. Personally, I am fine with such an inclusive definition, but most biologists are not. If artificial – man-made – life is to be considered truly life, then what is the principled distinction between life and non-life?

This broader problem with all attempts to answer "what is life?" becomes even more apparent when we consider the variety of "almost alive" parts of our universe. All of these border-line cases, described below, can be described as satisfying Clark's three-part definition. Yet none of these borderline cases is generally considered, by modern biologists, to be alive, revealing the intuitive and problematic approach to "life" that is implicit in modern biology and philosophy of biology.

Viruses are the most well-known member of this group of border-line cases. Viruses are responsible for the common cold and for the flu, as well as many other damaging diseases. Viruses are very simple creatures that consist of merely a protein shell and a dab of RNA, which is a precursor to DNA. Viruses can't reproduce without invading host cells and co-opting their reproduction machinery. A virus will attach itself to a cell wall, penetrate the wall and transfer its RNA into the cell. The RNA melds itself with the cell's DNA, forcing the cell to create more viruses. It's incredibly ingenious when we look at it with fresh eyes. How on Earth did such complex processes evolve in such tiny and apparently non-complex creatures? It's one of many marvels of life as we know it.

Yet many biologists consider viruses not to be alive. Or, to be more accurate, they consider a virus when it is in its dormant state outside of a host cell to be inert non-living matter. This is the case because the virus can't reproduce itself without invading a host cell. Thus it lacks a basic feature of almost every definition or description of life: the ability to reproduce itself. This distinction itself quickly becomes manifestly arbitrary, however, when we ponder why the distinction is drawn between a virus outside of a cell and a virus inside a cell. Once the virus is inside the cell, it loses any independent existence because its RNA melds with the DNA of the host cell. If the virus outside of the cell, with its little protein shell and RNA, is not alive, what suddenly becomes alive when it merges with the host cell? Is it now a virus/host combination entity that is alive? Or is the virus to be considered conceptually distinct even when it is attached to a host cell and its RNA injected into the host cell? If so, why? These lines of questioning should at least reveal some of the conceptual difficulties with applying the "life" label to certain things and not others.

Self-replicating RNA is a second type of border-line biological agent. Self-replicating RNA consists of only a strand of RNA. As the name suggests, it's different than normal RNA, which occurs inside cells, in that it can reproduce itself without a cell's help. Self-replicating RNA creates whole new strands of RNA as a free-floating agent outside of a cell. Is this life? Why not?

What about prions? Prions are self-replicating molecules responsible for various diseases such as "mad cow disease." Prions are even simpler than viruses and self-replicating RNA. Prions consist of nothing more than a very simple protein enfolded in a certain way. In fact, some definitions of "prion" refer only to the *information* about enfolding the protein, rather than the actual protein. Prions – a contraction of "protein infection" – infect normal proteins and cause them to fold in a way that is always lethal. In cows, the prion infects the brain and causes normal proteins to fold in such a way that it ruins the normal functioning of infected cells. Prions are like viruses in that they don't seem to have built-in reproductive machinery (and if the prion is simply information that directs the enfolding process it doesn't, by definition, have any "machinery" at all). Yet *something that we describe as a prion* does reproduce and its reproduction is the simplest type of reproduction possible. Prion reproduction is a simple transfer of information, consisting of the way the infected protein folds, from a prion to a normal protein. The act of transferring this information, however this is done at the microbiological level, is itself the prion's reproductive act. Indeed, it is the only reproduction possible for such a simple form, for what else would reproduction of a prion, a mere way of protein enfolding, consist of? We see, then, that the prion does in fact have its own reproductive machinery built into its very simple structure. Recent research has also found that prions evolve just like DNA-based life. So is a prion alive? If not, why not? It seems to meet Clark's three-part test.

This is the kind of difficulty that arises from any proposed definition of what is necessarily in flux. Aristotle, the world's first systematic biologist, solved this problem by realizing that *all things are alive to some degree.* Life is simply the flux of increasingly complex forms, which includes all matter in the universe. As matter becomes more complex, it becomes "more alive." An electron is alive, but just a tiny bit. A molecule of oxygen is alive, but just a little bit. A virus outside a cell is alive, but just a tiny bit, and a prion, and so on. There is a remarkable step upward in complexity with the advent of cell-based life, but there is still a continuum of complexity, of life, that includes this unusual and wonderful increase in life. Aristotle wrote, two and a half thousand years ago that "Nature proceeds little by little from things lifeless to animal life in such a way that it is impossible to determine the exact line of demarcation, nor on which side thereof an intermediate form should lie."

Aristotle's insight leads to an interesting conception of life when we pair it with Whitehead's process philosophy. As we've seen in previous chapters, Whitehead conceived of all matter as "drops of experience." A key feature (perhaps *the* feature) of this rudimentary experience is *will*, which includes at its most fundamental level the ability to make choices about how to move and how to manifest in each moment, given the tumult of available information from the surrounding universe. Whitehead, Schopenhauer, David Bohm, Freeman Dyson, Griffin, and others have suggested that all matter, even subatomic particles, has some freedom of choice over how to move and manifest in each moment. Dyson writes that "the processes of human consciousness differ only in degree but not in kind from the processes of choice between quantum states which we call 'chance' when made by electrons."

It is generally only in highly complex collections of matter, such as in forms that we consider alive in a traditional sense (cell-based life), that we see the *obvious* manifestations of this ability to make choices. But the choices are also manifest, as Dyson writes, in forms that we would not traditionally consider alive, such as atoms and subatomic particles, and very likely in macroscopic structures larger and more complex than humans.

J.B.S. Haldane, who puckishly refused to answer the question of what life is in his 1947 essay, supported the view that there is no clear demarcation line between what is alive and what is not: "We do not find obvious evidence of life or mind in so-called inert matter…; but if the scientific point of view is correct, we shall ultimately find them, at least in rudimentary form, all through the universe." More recently, University of Colorado astrobiologist Bruce Jakosky, who has worked with NASA in the search for extraterrestrial life, asked rhetorically: "Was there a distinct moment when Earth went from having no life to having life, as if a switch were flipped? The answer is 'probably not.'" Aristotle, Haldane and Jakosky are not alone, however, among eminent scientists in holding this view. Bohr, the eminent Danish physicist discussed in previous chapters, agreed, stating that the "very definitions of life and mechanics … are ultimately a matter of convenience…. [T]he question of a limitation of physics in biology would lose any meaning if, instead of distinguishing between living organisms and inanimate bodies, we extended the idea of life to all natural phenomena."

This argument shares many obvious similarities with the argument for panpsychism in earlier chapters – the idea that all things have some type of experience that becomes more complex as the organization of matter becomes more complex. We see now that "life" and "consciousness" may be viewed as different terms for much the same thing. As matter becomes more complex, it becomes more alive and more conscious. Consciousness refers to the inner subjective realm and life to the same process *when viewed from the outside.* In other words, consciousness is the view from inside and life the view from outside. Consciousness is about internal events and life about external observable behavior.

We reach, with this analysis, a clean synthesis of physics and biology. Physics is the science of fundamental physical forms, which are just a little bit alive, and which necessarily involves the study of space and time (the containers for form). Biology is, then, simply the science of *more complex life forms,* and in particular (but not always) cell-based life. The practical dividing line between these two fields becomes arbitrary and a matter of convenience or tradition.

Establishing what constitutes life is a perfect example of the inductive method and its difficulties. All definitions or lists of criteria for establishing the presence of "life" proceed from an intuition about what life is – begging the question it seeks to answer. If we are presented with a list of criteria for "life" we are prompted to ask why each criterion is offered and what would remain as a workable framework if any particular criterion was eliminated. This is what Clark attempts in his framework, in which he reduces the criteria to just three, down from as many as twenty or more in other lists. All of these lists, however, proceed from each biologist's intuition about what *should* be considered alive. And yet, as we see from an examination of the border-line cases, all such divisions become arbitrary. The solution to the problems of the inductive method, in this case and with science more generally, is to acknowledge that we are simply giving a name to a certain aspect of the universe ("life"), we are trying to describe that aspect, but we must acknowledge its existence as a continuum, not an all or nothing property of certain kinds of matter.

We are led in the final analysis to realize that Schrödinger was in fact right in his assertion that the defining characteristic of life is negentropy – a tendency toward order, toward increasingly complex forms and the maintenance of form. Life may be defined ultimately as *the process that creates and maintains form.* This is another way of stating Schrödinger's insights. We may extend Schrödinger's insights further by realizing that all parts of the universe share this characteristic to some degree.

Applying this definition, we may ask: does a virus "create and maintain form?" even when it hasn't co-opted a cell's reproductive machinery? The answer is clearly yes; thus a virus is a little bit alive in all phases of its lifecycle. Does self-replicating RNA create and maintain form? Obviously it does or we would have nothing that we could identify as the self-replicating RNA molecule. Thus self-replicating RNA is a little bit alive. Do prions create and maintain form? Clearly they do. Otherwise they would have no impact on their unfortunate victims in, for example, cows infected with mad cow disease. Thus, the set of molecular enfolding instructions that we call a prion is a little bit alive. Does the transition from water to ice create and maintain form? The answer is clearly "yes." Just a little bit. Does the simplest molecule of all, the hydrogen molecule that consists of two hydrogen atoms, create and maintain form? Again, the answer is clearly yes because we would otherwise have no identifiable thing we can call a hydrogen molecule. The order it maintains is itself. What about the hydrogen atom itself? Again, yes, it does create and maintain order through its own instantiation. The hydrogen atom consists of a neutron, proton and an electron. This is the simplest possible atom. Its existence is, by its identity as an atom, the creation and maintenance of form.

The whole universe is, thus, alive, through its constituents' creation and maintenance of form. But what about the universe as the sum of its constituents? Is the universe itself, as a unitary entity, alive? Under the definition offered here we must answer this question in the affirmative: the universe, through its manifold and obvious instantiations of form and maintenance of form, which allow us to exist and probe our wondrous milieu, is manifestly alive.

Evolution is an ascent toward consciousness.

Pierre Teilhard de Chardin (1959)

Chapter 22: Evolution is a basic principle of the universe

Life is constantly changing. Biological evolution (change) is undeniable. This biological truth was widely accepted before Darwin shattered the complacency of Victorian England in 1859 with his *On the Origin of Species*, with its controversial theory of natural selection. Darwin's major insight, rather than the fact of evolution itself, was to suggest a plausible mechanism to explain biological change, evolution. Darwin's book, along with the much lesser known work of Alfred Russel Wallace, forms the basis for modern biology, what is now known as the Modern Synthesis or neo-Darwinism. The Modern Synthesis consists of Darwin's ideas, expanded significantly since his time by other biologists, and the science of genetics, which arose a few decades after Darwin's major work.

Another of Darwin's concepts that should be as uncontroversial as the fact that life forms change over time is the idea of "common descent." This phrase merely means that all of today's species evolved from previous forms in one unbroken chain from the origin of DNA-based life on our planet (whenever that occurred).

The Modern Synthesis is quite simple at its core: random genetic variations occur through various means and some physical traits, based on genetic variation, lead to increased survival and reproductive success. The rewards in this grand game are more offspring bearing the parent's genes. The ultimate punishment is the lack of offspring that survive long enough to reproduce themselves.

When Darwin proposed his ideas in *On the Origin of Species* and in later books, they were met with incredulity by the majority of scientists as well as clergy throughout the "civilized" world. His ideas regarding evolution by natural selection, in particular, clashed with the prevailing views of biology and clashed most obviously with religious notions about the relationship between human beings, other animals and the theistic God of Christianity that had held sway in the Western world for over a thousand years.

Prior to Darwin, the prevailing biological theory of evolution – yes, there was a theory of evolution before Darwin – was the idea that acquired traits could be inherited. This theory was promoted most vigorously by Jean-Baptiste Lamarck (1744-1829), a French biologist, about fifty years before Darwin's major work was published in 1859. The theory of the inheritance of acquired traits, now generally known as Lamarckism, asserted that animals acquired traits in their lifetimes through, among other things, exertion and habit, such as the classic example of a giraffe reaching high for leaves, and thus acquiring a longer neck, or through repeated use of a tail for balance, leading to the muscular tail in kangaroos and wallabies. Lamarck held that acquired traits were in some cases passed on to offspring. We know, of course, that this is not how evolution occurs, but we'll see shortly that Lamarck wasn't entirely wrong.

Lamarckism clashes with the Modern Synthesis because what is known literally as the Central Dogma in the Modern Synthesis asserts that acquired changes never impact genes. Information flows only one way: from genes to bodies and never from bodies to genes. Darwin argued, in the first edition of On the Origin of Species, that, generally, only those traits that an organism started with could be passed on to offspring (this was not Darwin's final view on the matter, however, though this fact is often overlooked by modern biologists). Since Darwin's era we have learned much about inheritance and genetics – the molecular basis for genes was completely unknown in Darwin's time.

It has since become dogma that genes are generally the only basis for variation of traits, which are generally considered to be random. Random variations are then acted on by the process of natural selection, the survival of the fittest. The Central Dogma of the Modern Synthesis asserts that any somatic (bodily) changes to a given organism during its lifetime aren't incorporated into that organism's germ line (the complete genetic code for each organism that is contained in the sex cells, as opposed to the somatic cells). Only genetic changes that occur in sexual reproduction or from mistakes in copying the genetic code, the Central Dogma asserts, are passed on to offspring.

One problem with the Modern Synthesis, however, is its failure to convincingly explain how random processes lead to the breadth of useful mutations that have resulted in the amazing variety of highly specialized features we see in the natural world. Unfortunately, the Modern Synthesis has become, largely as a reaction to Creationism and its close cousin Intelligent Design, sometimes as dogmatic as its less scientific rivals in dealing with challenges to specific doctrines that form the Modern Synthesis.

It is helpful to think of the problem of random variation this way: at each step in the normal evolutionary process for any given genetic line, there are theoretically an infinite number of possible mutations that could occur in the genome. And yet, of the infinite possibilities, we witness over and over the occurrence of beneficial mutations. There are also countless neutral and non-beneficial mutations, which far outweigh the number of beneficial mutations. Mutations lead either to lower reproductive success, no reproductive success or simply the death of the organism. The majority of mutations are, however, neutral in impact, conferring no advantage or disadvantage on the life form and often not having any physical manifestation whatsoever. Much of our DNA is "junk" because it doesn't seem to encode anything important. This may be a symptom of our ignorance at the present time or it may really be just junk. But over the almost four billion years that life has existed on our planet, each step of the evolutionary drama, played out with every organism that has ever lived, has led to a sufficiently large number of beneficial mutations for nature to act upon and produce the amazing variety of adaptive features in today's organisms. As Darwin wrote: *"There is grandeur in this view of life.* From so simple a beginning, endless forms most beautiful and most wonderful have been, and are being evolved."

Darwin, having no knowledge of the specific biological basis for variation, simply asserted the existence of variation as the first step in his theory. Unfortunately, the details of how beneficial variations arise remain a key mystery in the Modern Synthesis. Some have attempted to calculate the probabilities involved regarding random beneficial mutations. Sir Peter Medawar, a British biologist and Nobel Prize winner in medicine, calculated the probability of random mutation leading to the variety of useful traits we see today as being infinitesimally small. Yes, three or four billion years is an immense length of time for life to develop on Earth. But it is not *infinite* time. According to Medawar's calculations, it would require near infinite time for life as we know it today to have evolved through a process of truly random mutation and natural selection acting upon this random variation. It is becoming increasingly clear that random variation isn't entirely random. There are very likely various mechanisms and process that dramatically reduce the possible variation in ways that facilitate beneficial variations/mutations. This is the topic of Kirschner and Gerhart's book, *The Plausibility of Life*, in which they discuss their theory of "facilitated variation." This theory argues for what I've just described, that most variation isn't entirely random and that the range of possible variation is far smaller than truly random variation.

We needn't, however, rely only on abstract reasoning to conclude that the Modern Synthesis is incomplete. Fortunately, we also have a growing treasure trove of data showing that non-genetic variation is inherited in many circumstances, and not merely through cultural transmission from parent to child. Again, the Central Dogma – the generally unchallenged and unchallengeable starting point for modern biology – holds that only germ line genetic variation is transmitted to the next generation. But there is undeniable evidence now available that shows that somatic variation is in many situations transferred into germ cell genes and thus passed on to the next generation.

A particularly interesting example is the green sea slug. This organism, hardly the favorite study object of modern biologists, has been found to pass key acquired traits to offspring. The green sea slug gets its name from the algae it eats. It literally becomes green because its skin becomes like a leaf, capable of photosynthesis. The green sea slug has the proud distinction of being perhaps the only animal that can survive on sunlight alone – once it ingests enough green algae to be able to manufacture its own chloroplasts, the little green power plants in leaves that turn sunlight into energy. If this wasn't interesting enough, the adult green sea slug can also pass this acquired trait, the ability to make its own chloroplasts, directly to offspring in just one generation. This seems to be a contradiction of the Central Dogma, revealing yet again the complexity and grandeur of life in all its forms.

Another interesting case of the inheritance of acquired traits involves smaller creatures known as *ciliates*. Ciliates are protists, fairly simple multicellular creatures, that live in the ocean. They are named after their *cilia*, small whip-like features that are used for swimming and feeding. The cilia typically have a "grain" to them, much like a cat or dog's hair has a grain to it. Experiments have found that a surgical reversal of a flap of skin on a ciliate's back will be reproduced faithfully in the ciliate's offspring. That is, an area of skin on the back of the ciliate is removed, turned around, and re-attached to the unwitting ciliate surgical patient. The result is that the creature's cilia face the opposite direction. This reversal of cilia direction is passed directly to offspring. This is, again, a contradiction of the Central Dogma. There are many other such examples. In sum, evidence is accumulating that Lamarck was in some ways right.

As with every chapter thus far, we must ask ourselves why does this matter? Why do arguably esoteric discussions of evolutionary biology matter to integrating science and spirituality, the main topic of this book? This discussion matters because of two things: 1) the centrality of the principle of evolution to modern science and increasingly to every aspect of our lives; 2) the degree to which the Modern Synthesis is still incomplete.

The principle of evolution is simply the idea that all things change and that some changes to whatever process is being examined will naturally spread. The principle of evolution is far broader than the Modern Synthesis, so my advocacy of the principle of evolution does not necessarily imply that I advocate the validity of the Modern Synthesis. As I just mentioned, the Modern Synthesis is incomplete, and may in fact be wrong in some aspects.

The principle of evolution applies to all processes, not just biological forms. Stated as it is here, the principle of evolution is unassailable in the same way a simple mathematical equation such as 2 + 2 = 4 is unassailable. It's about as certain as knowledge can be.

The principle of evolution is perhaps most obvious in the realm of ideas, of human thought. Richard Dawkins, probably the most prominent biologist alive in the early part of the 21st Century, coined the term "meme" in his classic 1976 work, *The Selfish Gene*. Dawkins is an "ultra-Darwinist" in that he views the Modern Synthesis, with its focus on evolution by natural selection, as for all practical purposes, the only agent of evolution. While I disagree with this point, his ideas about memes are highly relevant to cultural evolution. The meme is the thought-stuff equivalent of the gene – it is the unit that evolution acts upon in the realm of ideas. Changing memes lead to cultural evolution, and technological evolution, both of which are rapidly accelerating, to the delight of many and the dismay of some.

We can track the evolution of ideas, "memetic" evolution, by poring over books and other writings, architecture, art, conversation, and any other evidence left by human culture over the course of our history. The evidence of change and improvement is undeniable and obvious. Thomas McEvilley's 30-year labor of love, which resulted in his magnum opus, *The Shape of Ancient Thought*, can't be read by someone trained in biology (as I am) without seeing the obvious similarities in techniques between history and biology. McEvilley sifts through the written record for clues just the same way an anthropologist or paleontologist sifts through soil and rock looking for human artifacts or fossils. Both endeavors try to pull together tantalizing clues to create the broader narrative – and to determine how the subject of study has evolved over the millennia and eons. The principle of evolution is, thus, incontrovertibly part of every aspect of our existence.

The modern, unfortunately acerbic, debate over Intelligent Design and the Modern Synthesis revolves around the degree to which there is evidence of design in biology, a different matter than the more basic principle of evolution. The ongoing debate asks whether there are features of current or past life forms that simply can't be explained through the Modern Synthesis? This is not the place to hash out these issues in detail, but I will share my view that the current debate has become unnecessarily polarized. Moreover, it seems that Intelligent Design advocates ignore many lines of evidence that weaken their arguments and Modern Synthesis advocates are increasingly employing a scornful tone that achieves nothing good in this debate. Some of the more zealous defenders of the Modern Synthesis also too often pursue their own version of dogmatism – as revealed in the "official" name of the Central Dogma, and a too-quick dismissal of many lines of evidence that challenge aspects of the Modern Synthesis. Most generally, Modern Synthesis advocates ignore the role of consciousness/mind in the evolutionary process. I have fleshed out these ideas in my previous book, *Eco, Ego, Eros,* so will leave this discussion here and move on to more practical considerations.

*Science ... is becoming the study of
organisms. Biology is the study of the larger
organisms; whereas physics is the study of
the smaller organisms.*

Alfred North Whitehead, *Science and the Modern
World* (1925)

Chapter 23: Genes are not destiny

A little knowledge is a dangerous thing. It's even more dangerous when it *seems* that a little knowledge is a lot of knowledge. This is the case with modern biology. Due to the remarkable successes of the Modern Synthesis in explaining many things about the evolution of life, and the medical science that has arisen as a consequence, it is clear that we do understand many key features of complex life. Genetics as a science developed from Gregor Mendel's 19th Century investigations into pea cultivation. Mendel, an Austrian Augustinian monk, lived in Brno, in what is now the Czech Republic. Mendel's work included highly detailed and lengthy studies of pea reproduction. His work went largely un-noticed until the early years of the 20th Century, despite its relevance to Darwin's highly controversial theory of evolution described in his 1859 *On the Origin of Species*. Mendel found that certain traits, such as smoothness or bumpiness of peas, or the color of pea flowers, could be reliably predicted in later generations based on the traits of the parent peas. From these early insights, and Darwin's theory of evolution, the entire science of genetics developed.

Francis Crick and James Watson, British biologists, discovered the structure of the genes, which were found to be pieces of "deoxyribonucleic acid" – DNA. Crick and Watson's watershed discovery in 1953 earned them the

Nobel Prize and also ushered in a remarkable flood of discoveries regarding the nature of biology. In the early part of the 21st Century we learn about new discoveries, it seems with each week, of genes for various maladies or personality characteristics: genes for obesity, genes for depression, genes for intelligence, and so on.

As a result of these tremendous successes, it has become increasingly commonplace to attribute our personal successes and failures to genes. A runner breaks the world record in the 100 meter sprint and she will surely be described by some observers as having "good genes." Or if someone has aged well, it's because he or she has "good genes." It is not so fortunate when, on the opposite end of the spectrum, an obese person is given the ultimate free pass of being able to blame their genes.

I call this increasingly pervasive problem "genetic determinism." Perhaps the best statement of this sentiment was uttered by James Watson, the co-discoverer of the structure of DNA: "We used to think our fate was in our stars. Now we know in large measure our fate is in our genes." In the modern era of genetics and dramatically improved medical science, many people have succumbed to the idea that "it's all in our genes." Thankfully, this is not the case.

A relatively new science, known as epigenetics, has sprung up in the last two decades. The field of epigenetics studies heredity based on biological factors other than genes. The term "epigenetics" means "around the genes," so it examines features outside the genes that contribute to heredity. For example, the "scaffolding" of our chromosomes, known as histones, contains variations in form that lead to very different physical traits even though the underlying genes are identical. This is the case because histones control how chromosomes fold and thus what genes are accessible to the protein-manufacturing machinery of cells. So while the underlying genetic code could be identical, if the folding is different, the expressed proteins, and thus the organism itself, will be different.

This is just one of many well-studied epigenetic examples. Many modern biologists are still coming to terms with the fact that the amazing insights into the nature of genes and genetics can't explain heredity or evolution in full. It is perhaps surprising to those who are trained in today's neo-Darwinian school of thought, and its pervasive "genetic determinism," to find out how much heredity and evolution is based on factors other than genes.

Eva Jablonka and Marion Lamb deftly describe the various factors for heredity, which include genes and epigenetics, but also social and symbolic aspects, in their major 2005 work: *Evolution in Four Dimensions*. It is certainly the case that many heritable traits are determined largely by genes. For example, height, all other things (such as nutrition and child-rearing practices) being equal, is almost entirely a matter of the parents' genes. But my parenthetical caveat in the previous sentence also indicates that even something as apparently cut and dried as height is still subject to many non-genetic factors, including nutrition and child-rearing practices.

Genes are certainly not the full story, by any means, when it comes to heredity and evolution. We are not determined by our genes.

There is another very interesting new field of research that focuses on the impact of the mind on gene expression in individual humans. This is known as the "psychobiology of gene expression," and a book by the same title by Ernest Rossi, an American psychotherapist and author, cites numerous studies that find a strong link between mental or physical activity and how genes manifest in our bodies. Contrary to the generally accepted idea that our genes and the expression of those genes are fixed from birth, there is abundant and incontrovertible evidence that we may directly impact certain aspects of our gene expression in real-time. Let's look at an example.

So while our genetic code itself, our genome, changes very little during our lifetimes, in line with the Modern Synthesis of evolutionary theory, how our genome is *expressed in our bodies* at any given moment in time does in fact change. And this is not a widely known or accepted conclusion at this time. This change from orthodox biology is a very large window for a more empowered view of human health and psychology. We are far more in control of our bodies and our health than most of us realize. This control goes far beyond simply deciding what to eat or how much to exercise. We may, through learnable techniques, dramatically enhance our physical and mental well-being through conscious efforts to affect our particular gene expression in real-time.

This is an exciting new field, but like all new fields it will be some time before the more shaky conclusions are separated from the more rigorous findings. The study of human health, and techniques for enhancing human health, are areas that are particularly fraught with shaky conclusions because, I believe, of the very direct and powerful interest many people have in improving their health, beauty, intelligence, etc. We need worry less about charlatans in the fields of, for example, philosophy, than in human health because the former field is very lightly populated in comparison to human health and because academic philosophy doesn't seem to arouse the same kind of passion in the general public or the marketplace.

The unshakable conclusion, however, at this stage of our collective understanding, is that there is far more to heredity, evolution and human health than a simple decoding of genes and traits. Biology is far more complex than this, as suggested strongly by Jablonka and Lamb's *Evolution in Four Dimensions*, the growing field of epigenetics, and the even newer field of psychobiology.

While these developments in no way detract from the understanding of our true Self, and the comfort that this understanding brings, these new developments can take some of the sting of life away from our little selves – our constructed selves. By leading to less difficult lives as "mere" human beings, these developments in biology and psychobiology may also be helpful in leading all of us to the much grander truths about no-self and the true Self.

Chapter 24: Human evolution is just beginning

For all of our marvelous intentional adaptation to our various environments, human evolution is just beginning. We live in a very exciting time. We are on the cusp of transformative changes in how we work, play, love and even how we reproduce. These changes are made possible through our exponentially increasing knowledge of the natural world, of our bodies, and ever-increasing pace of technological change. This last trend is based primarily on one development: the modern computer. Who knew that manipulating zeros and ones, the two digits in binary code, could lead to such powerful changes? The increase in computer power since the 1950s has been staggering. "Moore's Law" is based on the observation that computing power doubles about every two years. This leads very quickly to huge numbers.

An old Indian fable illustrates this point very well. A talented inventor created the game of chess and brought it his king for approval. The king was very pleased at this exciting new game. He was so pleased that he asked the engineer how he would like to be paid. The inventor stated that he would like to be paid in rice. "Rice!" the emperor guffawed with incredulity. "Very well, how much rice would you like?" The inventor replied that he would like as much rice as it would take to place one grain on the first square of a chess board, which has 64 squares, twice that amount on the second, twice that amount again on the third, and so on. The emperor took the inventor for a fool and quickly agreed to this arrangement. It was only in the act of determining exactly how much rice this was, by actually following this simple "program" on a large chess board, that the emperor realized his mistake. Two to the 64th power is a very large number: 18,446,744,073,709,551,616. This is about 18 million million million. This is far more rice than exists on Earth today and far more than has ever existed or probably will ever exist.

Here's the point: doubling times of just two years, as we've seen with modern computing, yields rapid change. From the time when Moore's Law was first formulated in 1950 to 2010, the time of this writing, we have seen 30 doublings. This means computing power has increased by approximately one billion times (2 to the 30th power). This is why we can hold a powerful computer, a "smart phone," in the palm of our hand now and know that it has far more computing power than the largest mainframe computer of the 1960s.

But back to human evolution. Contrary to popular belief, human evolution has not stopped. Nor has it slowed down. It has in fact dramatically sped up since the advent of complex societies that were made possible by agriculture and other advances. Some studies have concluded that human evolution has sped up by a factor of 10,000 times or more when compared to non-agrarian society. Obviously, this change in the rate of evolution will lead relatively quickly to dramatic changes in our biology. Humans are far from finished with evolution.

Beyond "mere" biology, however, the far more significant type of human evolution is idea-based and technological, as suggested by the incredible growth of computing power. In the opening years of the 21st Century, the Internet and massive increase in personal computing have made us all veritable gods in terms of our ability to find and process information. We are now witnessing evolutionary changes – some would say revolutionary – that go far beyond information processing with the help of external devices. Prosthetic devices can now plug into nerve endings in lost limbs or even directly to our brains through various methods. Computers can "read minds" that are scanned by functional magnetic resonance imaging (fMRI), in a fairly rudimentary way at this point. For example, researchers at Carnegie Mellon University have succeeded in creating a software program that can state with high accuracy what object – a hammer, for example – a human subject is thinking about. It does not take much imagination to see where this rudimentary ability will lead. The clear trend in the not-too-distant future is toward integration of biological humanity with our own technological creations. Rather than having the Internet and all of its tools available on computers of ever shrinking size we shall surely soon have computer interfaces built in to our clothing, our jewelry, eyeglasses and probably even embedded in our brains before too long.

Many people contemplate such a future with dread. All technology is a double-edged sword. Indeed, all tools more generally are double-edged swords because all tools can be used for good or ill. I view technology as on balance a positive force in our lives, despite its many obvious downsides. Yes, technology gave us Hiroshima and Nagasaki, and the countless other brutalities made possible by guns, cannons and even longbows, spears and simple clubs. And technology is responsible for turning many people in our time into sedentary "couch potatoes" as they spend far too much time watching TV or playing video games. Yet the benefits of technology are too numerous to count. Broadly speaking, medical advances that have significantly extended the quality and span of human life, tools for exploring the very small (microscopes, etc.), the very large (telescopes, etc.), and the profound (atomic colliders, etc.), as well as the amazing entertainment and learning tools now available, seem to have on balance improved the lot of much of humanity. Our life spans are longer and we are generally healthier.

Whether we are happier or not is a more controversial question. The benefits of modern technology are, however, still far too limited in their geographic and social benefits, but if we can advance as far in our social, economic and governance systems as we have with our technological systems, it will not be too many more decades before all people on our humble planet share in the fruits of the technology. The "if" in the previous statement is, unfortunately, rather dubious at this point in time because it is far from certain that we will evolve our social and political institutions as fast as is needed.

I don't view technology from the point of view of a faith-based optimist. Indeed, I see tremendous problems looming on the horizon, not least of which are the threat of climate change and resource depletion ("peak oil" and the depletion of other fossil fuels, in particular). I am also increasingly worried about the problems of malicious artificial intelligence that may come up in the coming decades. These problems are beyond the scope of this book, but it is certainly my hope that by sharing the broad themes of this book, the central one being Self-realization – knowledge of our true Self – we will be more able to surmount these challenges as they arise.

The distractions of modern technology, one downside of our recent advancements, are not really different in kind than distractions available to people in every era. There have always been glitzy new toys and exciting new games and other pastimes. In every era. The Hindu stages of life framework recognizes this feature of reality. We are urged to explore hedonism early in life. Get rich. Enjoy all the toys we can. But before long we realize that these things are unfulfilling. It is only knowledge of our true Self, God-realization, that can provide lasting happiness and contentment. It is well worth quoting Yogananda again at this point: "Everything else can wait, but your search for God cannot wait." Insofar as technology distracts us from this goal, it can be damaging. But the alternative and valid view is that by making our material lives easier and more enjoyable we are also able to focus earlier and more seriously on Self-realization. If our future lives don't require working at crappy jobs for eight or more hours a day, vast possibilities are opened up in terms of finding the time for spiritual inquiry and enrichment, among many many other options for occupying our time.

Human evolution is just beginning. We will have many more distractions, some of which may keep us from Self-realization. But some options may help us in our true life's work. If we can pass the tests that face our infant species, challenges largely of our own making, we have a bright future.

Part VI: The nature of divinity

Divinity is less a *thing* than an attitude. The attitude of
divinity is to express reverence and sometimes awe. *What*
should be regarded with reverence and sometimes awe?
Ideally, all things should be so regarded. There are many
advantages to such an egalitarian approach to divinity – if it
is reflected in practice and not merely preached as an
ethereal but impractical spirituality. By regarding all things
as divine, we re-enchant our universe and ourselves.
Nothing remains "just" this or "just" that. *All of it becomes
endowed with some degree of enchantment.* This attitude
toward divinity may be intuited, deduced or simply
proposed as a working hypothesis, just as we have seen
with concepts such as consciousness, life and free will
discussed earlier. In fact, this attitude toward divinity, with
its own "pan" word, *panentheism* (the "en" in the middle
of this word is important in distinguishing it from
pantheism), provides a rigorous alternative to the
difficulties we face in mainstream religious views and in
mainstream anti-spiritual scientific views. This attitude
toward divinity is a result of looking at divinity as yet
another – but innately reverential – inquiry that is part and
parcel of our "deep science" approach that is central to
this book.

If divinity is an attitude, how are we to imbue this attitude
with some measure of practicality? If all things are to be

revered, how do we actually live our lives? Aren't some things still worthy of more reverence, even if the entire universe is in some sense divine? Arguably, yes, and it is for this reason that I describe further in the following chapters the "twin ultimates" that are perhaps worthy of particular reverence. These twin ultimates, God as Source and God as Summit, while worthy of reverence, certainly don't demand it. There is no angry God in this story. God is love, pure love. Pure bliss. Pure Creativity. And we are it. By revering God we honor and revere ourselves.

The universe is a collector and conservator, not of mechanical energy, but of persons. All round us, one by one, like a continual exhalation, 'souls' break away, carrying upwards their incommunicable load of consciousness. One by one, yet not in isolation.

Pierre Teilhard de Chardin (1959)

Chapter 25: God as Source and God as Summit are twin ultimates

What is the ultimate? And why do we strive toward it? Is there more than one ultimate? Is there an ultimate truth that we can discern either through reflection or through timeless spiritual teachings? A major theme of this book is humility. We must remain humble in the face of mystery and recognize that we shall never attain the ultimate truth; we shall, however, continue to strive toward truth and exploration of the ultimate. All things evolve. All things change. Modern religions shall unfortunately continue to clash with each other, and with scientific views, if they adhere to the notion of absolute and unchanging truth.

Any survey of human history, of intellectual history, of religious and spiritual history, reveals one thing: change. All actual things melt into dust, recombine in novel relationships, and evolve into something new. Change can be seen as its own ultimate – a recognition of the transience of life and all things in our lives. A certain comfort can arise from acceptance of this truth. In fact, Whitehead, one of my philosophical guides, makes Creativity, which is an advance into novelty in each moment, his foundational principle for his philosophical system.

Previous chapters delved into the nature of space, matter, energy, time and the ether, which I also call the ground/ocean of being and which modern science generally calls spacetime, the vacuum or the Grid. As we saw, space, the vacuum, is not really a vacuum. It is thriving, under our current physical theories, with fields, virtual particles and virtual energy. It is clear, regardless of prevailing physical theories, however, that *there is something that lies beneath, behind or within perceptible reality that is the deeper reality* than the world revealed directly to our senses or instruments. Without this hidden ocean of being we have nothing. Previous chapters discussed the "ether" from the perspective of physics. This chapter expands that discussion into the realm of spirituality.

The entire universe – the perceptible physical reality we live in – arises from the ocean of being, Source. The ocean of being is the metaphysical and physical origin from which all else emanates. It cannot be detected directly by us in the physical world, but its existence is known indirectly through numerous paths and occasionally experienced directly through God-realization. The ocean of being is very likely eternal (we'll never know) but it also is evolving over the course of unimaginable time. All manifest things change, so why not the ocean of being also? In order to produce and interact with manifest reality the underlying reality must also change. If it doesn't change in any way, how could it interact with, let alone produce, that which is always changing?

The ocean of being is equivalent to *Brahman* in Vedanta cosmology, Anaximander's *apeiron*, the Buddha's *Godhead* or *emptiness*, Plotinus's *One*, Jewish Kabbalah's *Ein Sof*, the Christian *creative* God, the Trinitarian Father, *purusha* in Hindu Samkhya, Whitehead's *creativity*, Jung's *unus mundus*, and in the most general sense simply *potentiality* – as discussed by Werner Heisenberg, Whitehead and many other physicists. Paul Tillich, the 20th Century Protestant theologian used the term "the ground of being" and described it as the "God above God." The conception of the ocean or ground of being I describe here has many similarities with Tillich's, but even more with Whitehead's ideas, known generally as "process philosophy."

All *actuality* – the manifest universe all around us – arises from the *potentiality* of the ocean of being. The ocean of being is the connection between apparently disconnected physical objects. Just as each island in a chain seems to be separate from its neighbor islands, but is in fact connected beneath the oceans to other islands and all other land masses on our planet, so the ocean of being connects all ostensibly separate things in the physical universe. *It's all just one thing*: the ocean of being and its emanations.

The ocean of being is not, however, necessarily the same as God. Words mean what we want them to mean and many have called Brahman and its conceptual equivalents "God," as just described. In the system I advocate, borrowing from Whitehead, Griffin, Ken Wilber and others, the ocean of being may be thought as Source – God as

Source. God as Summit, in my system, is a *consequence* of the ocean of being, not equivalent to the ocean of being. Source and Summit enclose all of reality within them. The ocean of being is the most basic *brute fact* that we simply accept, and appreciate, as the beginning of the great ontological chain of being. The ocean of being is where it all begins. Just as human consciousness arises from the interconnectedness of our constituent experiencing parts, however, all things, including God as Summit, arise from Brahman/Source. God as Summit is the *universal* consciousness. The physical universe is God's body *and* God's mind. The ocean of being is the substrate from which the physical universe and Summit emanate.

Mind and body are, in this story, complementary aspects of the same reality: inside and outside, subject and object. The *same* process that leads to the complex experience we humans enjoy leads to God's universal experience as Summit. God as Summit enjoys an experience that is the sum total of every experiencing entity in the universe, arising through the same holarchic process that creates consciousness at every level of reality. Whitehead, expressing one of the most comprehensive metaphysical truths, writes that "the many become one and are increased by one." This is the process that leads to a gnat's experience, a bat's experience, to your experience, to my experience and to God's experience. Earlier chapters described how all physical things are connected through the ocean of being. Just as ostensibly distinct atoms, molecules, cells, organisms, planets, and stars are in fact interconnected through the ether, the ocean of being, God's constituent parts are interconnected.

Does God as Summit actually exist? I don't know. Whereas I have had direct experience of God as Source, I remain agnostic about the existence of God as Summit. Perhaps our human destiny, in future eons, is to help bring God as Summit into being? How's that for a grand vision of our future? Regardless of God as Summit's existence now, my point in describing these concepts here is to suggest that the same process that leads to our minds may well lead to far greater minds than our own. And that process may well arrive at a universal mind, the mind of God. That's what I mean by God as Summit.

Source and Summit are *twin ultimates*. Either may be revered, but neither requires it. Ultimately, however, the *theory* of divinity, all the countless words we throw up into the air in our often-in-vain attempts at describing the universe, must yield to the *practicality* of divinity. How do we *live* in a way that allows us to know or participate in divinity? The practicality of divinity, in other words, the relationship of each of us to the divine, is the focus of the rest of this book. You needn't subscribe to my exact conceptualization of the divine to benefit from the other ideas I describe below. Your views could in fact diverge significantly from mine. Yet much of the *praxis* discussed later will still be of use. This is the case because it is up to each of us to create our conceptual framework, based on our unique experiences, learning, and intuitions. What may seem manifestly true to me may simply not work for you. It is not necessary, however, for complete agreement to be reached to arrive at useful insights and/or useful experiences. My primary goal in writing this book is to share my own insights regarding the integration of our various human selves with the true Self, and thereby help to improve integration in others and ultimately in society more broadly.

As always, we needn't and shouldn't take any conclusions on faith, including my own. Rather, we can and should always examine assertions for ourselves. We have various tools to probe deep spiritual realities, including meditation, travel, psychedelics, and discussion and reading. I urge you, gentle reader, to use what tools you are comfortable with to do your own explorations to examine my assertions.

Chapter 26: The Kingdom of God is within you

What is the Kingdom of God and where can we find it? The Kingdom of God is, to a Christian, the ultimate goal of the good life. More generally, we can use this term to express the goal of all religions: liberation and self-realization. While I focus on the Christian tradition in the following discussion, a similar analysis could be undertaken for most of today's mainstream (mainline) religions.

> Once, having been asked by the Pharisees when the kingdom of God would come, Jesus replied, "The kingdom of God does not come with your careful observation, nor will people say, 'Here it is,' or 'There it is,' because the kingdom of God is within you."

This passage, Luke 17:20-21, is a controversial Biblical passage to modern Christians because it contradicts one of the key creeds of almost every Christian tradition: that the Kingdom of God is outside of us and will be attained only upon death after having lived a virtuous life. But is the Kingdom of God up in heaven? Or is it within us now? Is it not yet discovered, but susceptible to discovery within us? Or is it a future kingdom that is more political than spiritual, a liberated and enlightened form of society that nurtures the downtrodden and the sick?

The most common view among Christians today, based on the New Testament and the 4th Century Nicene Creed, developed initially by the Egyptian Christian scholar Athanasius and the Roman Emperor Constantine, is that the Kingdom of God is in fact a realm to which believing Christians will be transported upon death, generally described as Heaven. In this view, the Kingdom of God is the Kingdom of Heaven. This is, to most people in the 21st Century who are trained in science or philosophy, a very difficult idea to accept. Is there really another realm in which our personalities, our souls, are transported to live in perpetual bliss, enjoying "eternal life"? There are so many seeming contradictions and conceptual difficulties with this view that I won't enumerate them here.

Another view that has achieved prominence, particularly in the developing world, is known as "liberation theology." Liberation theology focuses on the transformative effect of Jesus' message on how we treat each other in this life. The Kingdom of God is, in this view, a society governed by enlightened leaders who respect all people no matter what their social status, wealth, state of health, ethnicity or any other divisive category we care to apply. Jesus' message was overwhelmingly one of love – love for self, love for others, love for God. The Kingdom of God manifests naturally as a consequence of this love being lived and practiced by those who understand and accept Jesus' message. The Kingdom of God is most definitely not here now – we need to do a lot of collective work before we can realize this ideal society. Today's world is still overly war-torn, angry and unhappy.

A third view takes Luke's message more literally. The Kingdom of God is within us. It is not another realm we arrive at upon death. It is not a future earthly egalitarian kingdom we must collectively work for and hopefully realize one day. No, in this view, the Kingdom of God is achieved through *gnosis*, the realization of one's Godhood, what I have labeled "God-realization." By realizing that we are, each of us, God, we expand our limited human awareness to the awesome awareness of God. The part becomes the whole; or, more accurately, *the part finally realizes that it is inseparable from the whole and thus is more accurately identified as the whole than the part.* We manifest the Kingdom of God directly within us.

In this view, no church is necessary. No priests are required to interpret the confusing words of scripture. And *gnosis* puts each of us on a par with God and the ground of being. Or, again to be more accurate, we realize in *gnosis* that we *are* God and we always have been. We are Brahman "playing hide and seek with itself." We are awakened to our true nature. We are enlightened and liberated. We achieve *satori, samadhi, gnosis*.

This view seems radical to many because it is often interpreted as a way to avoid the entire system of sin, guilt and punishment built into almost every Christian tradition today. This is partly accurate. Believing that the Kingdom of God is within us does indeed eliminate the notion of sin – and the particularly damaging idea of "original sin" developed by St. Augustine and others early in the history of Christianity. Without sin, how are we to say what is correct behavior and what is not? Is God a punitive God or not? In the view of divinity I am outlining in this book, God is most definitely not a punitive God. God is not an entity that judges any one or any thing in the traditional Christian sense. We *are* God, even when we aren't actively realizing our own Godhood. Jesus' message, in this interpretation, becomes very simple: *find the Kingdom of God, our true identity, within yourself and act accordingly*. This is in fact all the spirituality we need. It is everything. How can we "sin" – harm others out of ignorance of our true nature – when we know that others are different manifestations of ourselves, that all apparent separation is only apparent? How can we mistreat our environment when we know that it is our body? Through this understanding of the Kingdom of God the "golden rule" – treat others as you would be treated – becomes much easier to live by.

"Love your neighbor as yourself" Christ tells us, echoing the Old Testament's similar admonition. Christ went even further in the Sermon on the Mount: "love your enemies" and: "If someone strikes you on the right cheek, turn to him the other also." Can we really live this way? Does anyone really live this way? These radical and seemingly impractical pronouncements become far less radical when we understand the Kingdom of God as *gnosis*. Indeed, once we make *gnosis* the first and foremost understanding of Christ's teachings, all other messages, including the difficult passages of the Sermon on the Mount, become relatively easy to understand. To *live* by these teachings is still, and shall remain, the more difficult task. To achieve this, regular practice is necessary.

There is unsurprisingly a long and controversial history behind this short discussion of the Kingdom of God. In the last decades of the 20th Century, new translations of the ancient writings found at Nag Hammadi in Egypt in 1945 became available. These writings, hidden in a large clay jar under the sand sometime in the 4th Century CE, are generally known as the "Gnostic Gospels." One of the original scholars who completed translations of these ancient documents in the 1970s, Elaine Pagels, wrote an accessible book by the same name in 1979. She described the interesting history of the early Christian church and the documents that eventually became known as the Christian Bible. The Gnostic movement was one of many spiritual movements inspired by Christ's teachings and life.

As often happens in the creation of "official" history, which is necessarily created after the fact by those who come victorious out of the fray, the Gnostic understanding of Christ's message became "heresy" only after an opposing Christian movement, led by Irenaeus, a bishop who lived in what is now Lyons, France, in the 2nd Century, and later by another bishop, Athanasius, in the 4th Century in Egypt, was successful in branding itself as "orthodoxy." This word means "right belief." *Beyond Belief: The Secret Gospel of Thomas* (2003) is Pagels' masterful follow up to her earlier book. *Beyond Belief* focuses in more detail on why and how the early church coalesced around a prescribed orthodoxy in the 4th Century, which formed the basis for much of present-day mainline Christianity. The early Christians faced tremendous persecution throughout the Mediterranean. They also faced constant disagreement from within the movement, which led to fracture and made them more susceptible to attack by opponents of any form of Christianity. Irenaeus wrote his major work, *Against Heresies*, around 180 CE, as a rebuttal against the Gnostic and other early Christian traditions that he viewed as wrongheaded. In fact, before the Gnostic Gospels were found at Nag Hammadi in 1945, most of what we knew about the Gnostic movement came from Irenaeus, its leading opponent.

The Gospel of Thomas, Gospel of Truth, Gospel of Mary, and other Gnostic gospels (none of which are in the current version of the Bible) present the teachings of Jesus, contrary to Irenaeus' preferred interpretations, in a way that makes *gnosis* the obvious and primary teaching. These gospels are acknowledged by all serious scholars as authentic even though they were not included in the Bible we know today. The remaining debate concerns whether these heterodox (heretical) teachings are closer to what Jesus really taught or, instead, the mainline teachings of Irenaeus and Athanasius are the more accurate view.

The Nicene Creed presents the mainline view that is common to the large majority of Christian denominations today. The most overt message in the 4th Century Nicene Creed is that Jesus was the only begotten Son of God, essentially on a par with God. Christ and God are two aspects of the same entity. The version of the Creed that is most common today states:

> We believe in one God, the Father Almighty,
> Maker of heaven and earth, and of all
> things visible and invisible. And in one Lord
> Jesus Christ, the only-begotten Son of God,
> begotten of the Father before all worlds,
> Light of Light, very God of very God,
> begotten, not made, being of one
> substance with the Father.

We know that the Creed was formulated in large part as a response to the teachings of a Libyan theologian, Arias, in the early 4th Century. Arias taught that Christ was created by God, and that, therefore, there was a time when Christ did not exist. This was considered by Athanasius and the large majority of other Christian leaders to be heretical. Emperor Constantine, as a direct response to Arias' teachings, convened the Council of Nicaea in 325 CE to establish what is now known as the orthodox view. Bishops from all over the Mediterranean region, including Athanasius, converged on this small town in what is modern-day Turkey. After much discussion, they actually voted on the final text of the Nicene Creed, voting overwhelmingly for the view that Christ was the Son of God, divine, and was to be considered essentially the same as God himself, but having taken human form.

Gnostic teachings, such as those contained in the Gospels of Thomas, Mary, Judas and Philip, to the contrary, all support in various ways the concept of the Kingdom of God within. In this view, Jesus was not the Son of God in an exclusive sense. According to these Gospels, Jesus never claimed to be divine in a way that made him different than other humans. Even in John, a key gospel for mainline Christians and the only one of the four standard gospels that includes Jesus' own claims to be divine, Jesus states:

> My prayer is not for them alone. I pray also
> for those who will believe in me through
> their message, that all of them may be one,
> Father, just as you are in me and I am in
> you. May they also be in us so that the
> world may believe that you have sent me. I
> have given them the glory that you gave
> me, that they may be one as we are one: I in
> them and you in me. May they be brought
> to complete unity to let the world know
> that you sent me and have loved them even
> as you have loved me.

This passage supports the Gnostic tradition, yet the very next passage in the Gospel of John states that God loved Christ "before the creation of the world," apparently contradicting again the Gnostic interpretation. Citing scripture is always tricky because of the confusing and often contradictory statements in the Bible, between the Old and New Testaments, between books in each testament and sometimes within books themselves. Bart Ehrman describes these difficulties of translation, interpretation and exegesis with grace and wit in his books *Misquoting Jesus: The Story Behind Who Changed the Bible and Why* (2005), *Jesus, Interrupted: Revealing the Hidden Contradictions in the Bible (And Why We Don't Know About Them)* (2009), and many other accessible works. The fact that most of the Bible was originally written in ancient Greek and then translated and transcribed countless times before arriving at what we have today is a significant source of the confusing nature of modern scripture.

In the face of this confusing and often contradictory evidence, what gives me personal faith that Jesus was a Gnostic is the universality of *gnosis* among great spiritual leaders. *Gnosis* is the basis for almost every tradition, including early Christianity, the Sufi tradition in Islam, Kabbalah in Judaism, and more overtly in Hinduism and Buddhism. *Gnosis* seems to have been the personal experience that inspired every great spiritual teacher. Unfortunately, less noble leanings quickly become mixed in with this divine inspiration and mainline religious traditions become over time more about power than God-realization. The next chapter explores this history in more detail.

If there were no real internal propensity to unite, even at a prodigiously rudimentary level – indeed in the molecule itself – it would be physically impossible for love to appear higher up, with us in 'hominized' form.

Pierre Teilhard de Chardin (1955)

Chapter 27: God is Love

This chapter again focuses on Christianity because it is the primary tradition in my particular slice of human history: 21st Century United States of America. My personal experience with Christianity has been conflicted. I grew up in a non-religious family, attending church only very occasionally. I don't recall a single family discussion about religion or spirituality while I was growing up. I did, however, acquire from an early age an aversion to religion, partly through my experience living for a year, in the early 1980s (without my parents), in a Jewish-Christian commune in Washington State. Many of the key leaders of this commune were Jewish, but the Christian Bible was presented as the key text. Love, the leader of the "Love Family," was a charismatic leader who exemplified well the perils of the 1960s counter-culture. After attracting a following at the various outposts of the Love Family, in Seattle, Arlington and a few other locations in Eastern Washington, Love seems to have been corrupted by his own power. A major split in the commune occurred when other leaders finally had enough of Love using donated funds to purchase drugs and his habit of sleeping with many of the women who joined the commune. Even at my young age – I was ten when I left the commune – I was left with a bad taste in my mouth with respect to religion and spirituality.

I continued to think, talk, meditate and read, however, and after going through various stages of agnosticism, atheism and other isms, I came to the realization that there is much truth in mainline religions and other, more amorphous, spiritual traditions. I was particularly attracted to Buddhism in my early 20s and have continued to be attracted to this loving and compassionate spirituality. I continued to explore, however, and came to realize that all spiritual traditions have much to offer and that what may seem like contradictions between traditions may often be resolved through deeper understandings that see past the particular words that may give the appearance of conflict or contradiction.

The deepest truth, revealed to us through the faith/reason complementarity, is that God is love and we are it. This is, again, *gnosis*, to use just one of the many terms for this experience/realization. This is both a metaphysical and highly practical truth. This is truth we can use.

Why is God love? God is love because being itself is pure bliss, another word for love. Brahman is, in the Hindu Vedanta tradition, "being, knowledge, bliss," *satcitananda*. All things are ultimately united in Brahman. The perceptible world is the emanation of Brahman, the dream of Brahman. When we see beneath the veils of the manifest world – *maya* – we experience Brahman directly. In *gnosis*, we experience Brahman, our true Self, as pure bliss. Through this experience we gain direct confirmation, as direct and incontrovertible as any knowledge can possibly be, that the ocean of being, Brahman, Source, is indeed pure love. Why is there something rather than nothing? Because Brahman, as pure love, offers up the world of multiplicity, of perceptible reality. But Brahman also offers us a way to see through the multiplicity to the deeper reality. Both are endlessly fascinating, but the deeper reality of Brahman offers the bliss that comes from attaining God-consciousness, the realization that we are Brahman.

Valentinus – not to be confused with the patron saint of Valentine's Day – was an early Gnostic theologian born in Egypt. He split from the church of his day after being passed over for a promotion to bishop. He is generally credited with authorship of the *Gospel of Truth*, one of the key Gnostic gospels found in 1945 at Nag Hammadi. Prior to this discovery, practically all that was known of Valentinus was through the highly critical discussion of his work and ideas in books by Irenaeus, Tertullian, and other proto-Orthodox theologians in the 2nd Century CE and later.

Valentinus describes a cosmology that is hard for the modern mind to accept because it is so mystical and seemingly distant from our modern world. But we need not accept the cosmology whole cloth (or any of it for that matter) in order to appreciate some of its wisdom. This is the case with all traditions. The *Gospel of Truth* urges: "Speak concerning the truth to those who seek it and of knowledge to those who, in their error, have committed sin. Make sure-footed those who stumble and stretch forth your hands to the sick. Nourish the hungry and set at ease those who are troubled. Foster men who love." God was, for Valentinus, a loving God. This is no surprise. How can perfect Self-knowledge not be loving? I am God, you are God, we are God. I am love, you are love, we are love.

The greatest romance you can have is the romance with God.... He is the Lover and our souls are the beloved, and when the soul meets the greatest Lover of the universe, then the eternal romance begins. The love that you have been seeking for incarnations through all human loves is at last yours.

20th Century Indian mystic Yogananda Paramahansa

Chapter 28: The Kingdom of God is outside you

Love transcends power. Yet power politics almost always seems to find its way into successful spiritual traditions. More often than not, once a spiritual tradition becomes a "religion" – due to its longevity, political success and/or the number of its members – it becomes more about power than about spirituality. The perpetual challenge for all spiritual traditions is to preserve the teaching that God is love, and we are it, in the face of far more mundane and less noble power politics. This teaching is all that is needed for a complete spirituality. The rest is embroidery.

Unfortunately, this essential message is often obscured or even lost entirely in mainline traditions. For example, we can't, with fresh eyes, read the book of Genesis and not see its author's transparent effort to wield God's word as a tool for increasing control of men over women and of rulers over both men and women. Genesis is both a creation myth and the first book describing the Mosaic Code, generally known as the Torah or Pentateuch, which consists primarily of hundreds (613 by one count) of commandments passed down by Moses and other prophets. Genesis, in its creation myth, describes God's creation of Adam and his later creation of Eve to serve Adam. Eve was weaker than Adam and quickly contravened God's commandment to not eat from the Tree of Knowledge. Not only did Eve disobey God's commandment, she convinced Adam to also eat from the Tree. God was not pleased and called down all manner of curses upon his disobedient creations.

The God of the Old Testament is often angry, vindictive, and cruel. There is little love to be found in Him. He is a transparently anthropomorphic patriarchal God designed by men to ensure obedience to the leaders of the early Jewish tribes in the face of great adversity from without and perhaps challenges to power from within. The God of the Old Testament, likely based *originally* on the profound *gnosis* common to all spiritual traditions, by the time that the books of the Old Testament were written, had long since been corrupted by power politics.

In the early history of the Jewish tradition, law and spirituality were one and the same. This is the case, in fact, in almost all traditions, not just Judaism. Law is, by definition, about power. Laws exist to guide and dictate allowable behavior. The book of Leviticus alone contains 247 commandments. Some are as seemingly innocuous but strange as forbidding followers from wearing clothing consisting of more than one type of fabric. Others are less innocent, describing the many infractions that are punishable with death by stoning. For example, Leviticus, Chapter 20, lists a number of laws, violations of which are punishable by death, including cursing one's parents, adultery, and sleeping with animals or a man sleeping with another man. If a man marries both a woman and her mother, "he and they must be burned in the fire." These laws clearly have little relevance to 21st Century behavior or ethics, let alone deep spirituality. Even more disturbing passages are common in the Old Testament. Psalm 137, a plaintive song against the oppression of the Jews by the Babylonians, ends with the horrific lines:

> O Daughter of Babylon, doomed to destruction,
> happy is he who repays you
> for what you have done to us --
> he who seizes your infants
> and dashes them against the rocks.

This kind of behavior was very likely widespread in the ancient world. Indeed, the Hindu tradition, recounted in many extremely long epics like the *Mahabharata*, describe numerous examples of human and divine brutality. Over time, cultures and religions have evolved to the point where passages like these are wisely ignored as atavistic and brutal vestiges of a much earlier and outdated period in human history.

Jesus himself was a major force in this evolution in the Western world. While reading the New Testament on this issue leads yet again to many conflicting interpretations of what Jesus "really" meant, it is clear from many sources that he was motivated first and foremost by an overwhelming compassion and concern for the most unfortunate in human society. Albert Nolan, a South African Catholic bishop, makes a convincing case in *Jesus Before Christianity* that Jesus was mostly concerned about the salvation of the majority in his culture, those who were not wealthy or educated. In 1ˢᵗ Century Palestine, like all cultures at the time, the large majority of people were not educated or wealthy. Nolan writes that the "poor and the oppressed and anyone else who was not too hung up on 'respectability' found the company of Jesus a liberating experience of sheer joy." Jesus "not only healed them and forgave them, he also dispelled their fears and relieved them of their worries. His very presence had liberated them."

Nolan, as a leading "liberation theologist," sees Jesus' primary message as salvation in this life, on this Earth. The Kingdom of God is achievable in the real world, if only Jesus' message can be internalized by enough people. Through faith in Christ and his message, Nolan believes, the Kingdom of God shall be realized here in this world. He believes that the key passage of Luke 17:21 has been misinterpreted by those, like me, who believe it is strong support for the Gnostic interpretation of Christ's teachings. Rather than being translated as "the Kingdom of God is within you," the traditional translation, it should be "the Kingdom of God is in your midst." Nolan's arguments are not convincing on this sub-issue, and ultimately it isn't important whether he is right or not on this particular issue of scriptural translation and interpretation because the Gnostic view of Christ's teachings and the liberation theology view can easily be reconciled.

The Kingdom of God within us does not exclude the liberation theology view that the Kingdom of God is a worldly kingdom. Rather, the Gnostic understanding of God within will do much to *hasten* the Kingdom of God on Earth. It will also do much to ensure that the Kingdom of God is not a kingdom but, instead, a democracy. For this is the key message of the Gnostic Jesus: we are, each of us, God, and we are, each of us, thus responsible for our own behavior and there is no "authority" higher than our Self – the true Self, not the little self. This is a radically democratic message. As human societies have evolved toward increasingly democratic systems of governance, so spiritual understandings have evolved toward greater spiritual democracy. The countervailing trend is the ever-present tendency of many religious leaders to subvert the inherent spiritual democracy of *gnosis* by imposing church dogma on top of the unadulterated and pure experience of God-consciousness.

Pierre Teilhard de Chardin, a brilliant Jesuit monk and paleontologist, described in his 1955 masterpiece, *The Phenomenon of Man,* the evolution of both matter and spirit, which are for him twin aspects of the same underlying reality. This process culminates in perfect unity, what he calls the Omega Point. This can be considered the Kingdom of God on earth *and* within us. Indeed, it requires this dual manifestation. It is worth quoting Teilhard de Chardin at length because, as a devout Christian with extensive training in biology and paleontology he was one

of a few thinkers in the 20th Century capable of
synthesizing science and spirit in a satisfactory way, which
transcends the Christian tradition he wrote within:

> As early as in St. Paul and St. John we read
> that to create, to fulfill and to purify the
> world is, for God, to unify it by uniting it
> organically with himself. How does he unify
> it? By partially immersing himself in things,
> by becoming "element," and then, from
> this vantage point in the heart of the
> matter, assuming the control and
> leadership of what we now call evolution.
> Christ, principle of universal vitality because
> sprung up as man among men, put himself
> in the position (maintained ever since) to
> subdue under himself, to purify, to direct
> and superanimate the general ascent of
> consciousness into which he inserted
> himself.... Then, as St. Paul tells us, *God
> shall be all in all.*

Part VII: Being a human becoming

What really matters to us, as human beings, is not theory. Theory is just a pointer. And it's not even "direct pointing," the key teaching method of Zen Buddhism, which attempts to get below the level of words and concepts to show students the underlying reality. Theory is perhaps, at best, a pointer to direct pointing. The remaining chapters of this book attempt to put the reader on a path to finding her or his own practice for experiencing and living *gnosis*. They are, unfortunately, yet more words. Alas, this is the nature of books; they are collections of words. My hope is that these final words will show why the theory covered in previous chapters may be helpful – and why we must eventually transcend theory.

Chapter 29: Be here now and enjoy the bliss within you

We human beings would be better described as "human becomings." As with all things in the universe, we are in constant flux. We are processes, not things. All we can know, literally, is one ever-present and continuous *now*. The past consists only of memories. The future consists only of imagination. There is only now. Even though the nature of reality requires that we live only now, and now, and now, however, we too often live in the past or the future – in our minds. The past may only be memories, but those memories can seem very real to us here in the present. Despite the fact that the future exists only in imagination, possible futures can still seem very real, inspiring fear or hope as the case may be.

There is an intellectual bliss that comes from God-realization, when we think through the rational consequences of the various chains of reasoning outlined here. This intellectual bliss can lead to a more visceral level of bliss if a deeper *gnosis* is achieved through such contemplation. This path to God is known in the Vedanta Hindu tradition and Buddhism as *jnana yoga*, the intellectual's route to God.

There are many other paths to bliss, some of which are more fundamental than the intellectual path. One readily learnable path springs directly from being here now. It is the simple experience of *feeling* one's body, feeling the somatic pleasure of pure being, having a corporeal form, our bodies, at the same time as we concentrate on the eternity of the present moment. In this readily available practice, we stop what we are doing and simply exist. We close our eyes and look within. We feel our senses, our bodies, our cells. We feel it all and revel in the present moment. The result is pure bliss.

We can't say what "really" gives rise to this bliss within us, but we can be satisfied at many levels in simply realizing the bliss is there, accessing it, and appreciating it. It is most likely the pure bliss of being in its various forms, which combine at many levels within us into the sum total of our bodies, which then give rise to our little selves. By seeking within, below the level of our senses and the phenomenal world more generally, we can find this bliss at almost any time. This somatic bliss is a taste of the true Self.

As with most features of our universe, *gnosis/Samadhi/satori* is not an all or nothing event. It comes in various shades. Rare are the occasions in which complete God-realization is attained for any sustained length of time. This is known in Vedanta as *nirvikalpa Samadhi*, which is the experience of Brahman beyond all form. This is direct and unadulterated merging of the little self with the larger Self, Brahman. More accurately, there is not really any merger because there is no separation to begin with. The *apparent* merger springs from the realization that there is no separation. With this realization, the tiny but all-important switch is made from duality to non-duality. We are re-born into our Self. In the Buddhist tradition, the historical Buddha is said to have achieved "unexcelled complete awakening" as he sat beneath the bodhi tree. In this awakening, Buddha became the universe – more accurately, he realized he was the universe. And always has been.

God-realization also comes in less profound forms, one of which I've just described as the somatic bliss of meditation. By peering within and experiencing, even for a short moment, the bliss that is our somatic blessing, we realize God for a small moment. With some practice this state can be attained in almost any setting and can be extended to many moments. And from this mini-*gnosis* that all of us can readily access, the full-blown *gnosis* that Buddha, Christ, the Sufi mystics and other mystics of all traditions have experienced and transmitted orally and in writing, may eventually be experienced by all of us. It's all a matter of degree.

Meditation is, of course, the traditional way to stop, look within and find this bliss. Alan Watts describes meditation as "the discovery that the point of life is always arrived at in the immediate moment." Indeed, all of life can only be lived in the present moment. We just don't generally realize this. Meditation can help bring our minds in line with reality by highlighting this point. Meditation is practiced in some form in almost every spiritual tradition. It is highlighted in the mystical traditions, for obvious reasons. The details of the various types of meditation are beyond the scope of this book.

A more limited framing of "be here now" is the ancient saying that "this too shall pass." "This too shall pass" can be helpful when the world seems to conspire against us. Indeed, all things do pass, but relying on "this too shall pass" during times that seem hard assumes judgments that aren't always valid. We have an in-built tendency to judge events as "good" or "bad," to put it very simply. We don't need to think about these judgments; they are instinctual and usually immediate. Such judgments assume, however, that we actually know what good and bad are and that such judgments made on the spot are valid then and will remain valid in some semi-permanent sense. It's easy to see, when we think through a simple example, that judging what is good and bad is not very accurate and generally not very helpful for living our lives in a fulfilling way. The classic Chinese Taoist way of making this point goes like this.

A Chinese farmer and his son shared a small plot of land. A horse jumped their fence to graze on their land. The law at that time dictated that a horse that came onto one's property unattended by its owner became the landowner's property. Horses were generally only owned by wealthy families and having a horse was a major status symbol. The son was ecstatic at this good fortune. The father, knowing a bit better, cautioned his son: "Who knows what is good and what is bad?" The next day the horse jumped over the fence the other way and galloped away, causing the son to get upset at this bad luck. The father repeated his admonition. The next day, the horse returned, this time with a dozen wild horses as companions. The son was once again ecstatic at this great good fortune. The father repeated his admonition. The next day the son attempted to ride one of the wild horses and was thrown to the ground, breaking his leg. The father repeated his tired question: "who knows what is good and what is bad?" The next day the local warlord arrived and demanded that every young able-bodied man join his army to fight the neighboring warlord. The son was relieved to be passed over due to his broken leg.

And so on, with every event that happens in our lives.

We never know what is good or bad because these judgments are a matter of timescale and the limited point of view that we bring to bear in our judgment. We must reserve judgment until the very last breath we draw. And even then we realize, based on the discussion in previous chapters, that we still won't know at the point of bodily death what is truly good or bad because our bodily death is insignificant in terms of the true Self. The grand evolutionary trend in the universe is toward greater complexity, toward greater knowledge of Self because of the evolutionary principle working its magic, aided by the inherent consciousness within all things. This is the only "good" thing we need truly concern ourselves with. The rest is detail that, while interesting, shouldn't cause us too much grief or elation. The more appropriate attitude to life's vicissitudes is to dance with events as they take us in their grip. Appreciate everything here and now, even those events that seem at the time to be "bad." Almost every situation has some silver lining and we ultimately never know what is good or bad.

A key part of knowing your Self is the trained ability to peer within at any moment and find that peace, that bliss, that lies within us at all times. Feel your senses, go below them, feel the happy humming of your cells, your molecules, your atoms. Be here now. This very simple act is knowing thy Self. It is the basic experiential complement to the intellectual knowledge of Self. The experiential and the intellectual combine into one in this act, this mini-*gnosis*.

What about larger human trends and man's ongoing inhumanity to man and our environment, those things that we can very easily label as "bad"? Should we approach human barbarity and injustice with the same kind of equanimity and reserve of judgment? There is certainly a level at which these things should be treated in the same way as the tale of the farmer and his son. Who knows what is truly good and what is truly bad? Yet we cannot lose sight of our humanity out of obedience to purely cosmic principles and a desire to seek our true Self, at the cost of our humanity. We must, as human beings, find a balance. We are embodied beings and we cannot ignore our biology and our social selves, our little selves. Even these little selves are part of the true Self. Indeed, all great spiritual teachers have resisted the temptation to retreat to the high mountain caves and pursue divine contemplation free from the distractions of "mere" human affairs. To integrate our various aspects, we must show compassion for our fellow beings – all of our fellow beings, not just human beings. At times, this can and should include political activism.

Jesus and Buddha's basic message was simple: know thyself and the rest will follow. Yes, when we know our true Self we cannot help but love our neighbors and our enemies as we love our little self: my neighbor is my Self, my enemy is my Self, so how can I not love my Self? This is all the spirituality we really need. More complex teachings develop in every tradition, despite this essential teaching's completeness, because the simplicity of this message is often obscured by power politics and rival teachings. Know thy Self. That's it.

Problems also occur when others around us, who we cannot ignore, don't realize their true Self. Our role as tasters of *gnosis*, as those who have attained some level of God-realization, even the mini-*gnosis* available by feeling the somatic bliss within us, is to pursue our own lives in such a way that we help others attain this same realization. This is the Bodhisattva's path in Buddhism – the refusal to retreat to the mountain top until every last blade of grass realizes it too is God. This is the balance we must find as we pursue our own paths to greater and greater God-realization – without forgetting our humanity.

To see a world in a grain of sand,
And a heaven in a wild flower,
Hold infinity in the palm of your hand,
And eternity in an hour.

18th Century English poet William Blake

Chapter 30: Everyone needs a praxis

"Be here now" is one very simple, yet powerful, example of a *praxis* – a spiritual practice designed to achieve God-realization. Be Here Now may be considered a complete praxis in itself, despite its simplicity. As discussed, it is the entryway for knowing your Self, which is the core spiritual teaching in every mystical tradition. With practice, this entryway may be enlarged to constitute all spiritual truths. But we humans are all different. Some of us are more receptive to imagery, some to sounds, some to words and intellectual discussion, some to direct visceral experience. It is for this reason that most spiritual systems have developed various ways of teaching their essential message. I take the Hindu/Buddhist descriptions as a sample taxonomy of the kinds of paths to God that are available – there are surely many other ways to describe the many paths to God, but the Hindu/Buddhist taxonomy is simple and full of truth. Each of these paths is a *praxis*. They are not mutually exclusive.

The traditional description includes four paths to God: 1) *jnana yoga*, the intellectual path to God; 2) *karma yoga*, the path of good works exemplified by Mother Teresa and countless others like her; 3) *bhakti yoga*, the path of devotion to a particular realized figure such as Christ, Buddha, Krishna, etc.; 4) *raja yoga*, the path described by Patanjali in his *yoga sutras*, a set of sayings written down sometime prior to 500 CE. We can dispense with the fourth category in our discussion because it's not really a different-in-kind system from the first three (Indian systems often involve four categories as a default preference even if there is little justification for four items).

It will be no surprise to the reader that this book follows most strongly in the *jnana yoga* tradition. A prominent text in this tradition, entitled *Jnana Yoga*, was written by Swami Vivekananda in the late 19th Century. Vivekananda was a tireless Indian scholar and teacher who made it his life's work to share the rich Indian spiritual tradition with the western world. His life was lived in the *karma yoga* tradition, though he wrote extensively about all four of the yoga traditions. *Jnana yoga*'s primary developer was, however, Shankara, who lived in India in the 8th Century CE. Shankara's main work is *The Crest-Jewel of Discrimination*. Shankara stressed the non-duality of all things and claimed that his path was the fastest path to God-realization. He had a tendency to downplay the importance of other paths. *Jnana* can lead directly to God-realization, but it will more likely be the primer, the entry way, for a more visceral type of understanding for most people. *Jnana* is, as this book is, a pointer to direct pointing, to the underlying reality of Brahman/Source/God.

Karma yoga is the path to God that relies on tireless devotion to improving the lot of others in this world. Through selfless behavior, the little self is expanded to the point where the true Self may be realized. It is through action, in this tradition, that God-realization is achieved. Indeed, the very acts of devotion constitute God-realization. One doesn't need to have the traditional experience of "seeing God" as a bright light and bathing in pure bliss to achieve God-realization. This is certainly the prototypical *gnosis* mystical experience, described throughout the spiritual literature in all cultures and in many works of literature by poets and mystics. But not all of us are so fortunate to enjoy this level of profound experience. We may ultimately achieve the same results through good works and devotion to others – if it is genuine devotion that we pursue. There are many paths to God.

The *Bhagavad Gita* is the primary text in the Hindu tradition of *karma yoga*, though it also has much to say about other yogas. It is a tale of Arjuna, a young nobleman facing his family and friends on the battlefield as he struggles with his various duties. Krishna is Arjuna's charioteer, both a human friend and an avatar of God itself who incarnates in each age to advise us on how to live in accordance with cosmic law. Krishna advises Arjuna on his roles in life, his *dharma*, his true Self, and many other topics. There are some teachings of the Gita that are outdated, such as the Gita's emphasis on performing our assigned roles in life, based on our karma-ordained *dharma*, even if it requires killing our brothers on the battlefield, which is the background storyline in the Gita. Moreover, there is little room for free will in the world of the Gita. Yet despite these particularly uncomfortable teachings, many of the teachings of the Gita translate seamlessly into the modern world and the broader trends of spiritual democracy and *gnosis*. For this reason it remains one of the beloved texts of the rich and ancient Hindu tradition.

Christ himself is a wonderful example of a devotee of *karma yoga*, as is the Buddha, though Christ taught little about *dharma* in the sense of ordained roles in life. As discussed above, Christ's first and foremost message was *gnosis*, if we treat the Gnostic tradition as the most pure transmission of Christ's teachings. *Gnosis* is the basis for Christ's admonition to "love thy enemy" and to "turn the other cheek." It was this understanding that led Christ to work for the entirety of his short life to improve the lot of the poor and the dispossessed in his society. Yet even if we look to the traditional gospels of the New Testament, the same message of compassion and tireless work comes through strongly. Christ's life and message were designed to improve the lot of all people, but particularly the lowliest among us. The "last shall be first," and the "meek shall inherit the Earth." It was Christ's singular mission to lose himself through service to others, and thus to regain his true Self, while acting as an example to others for finding their true Self.

Bhakti yoga appeals to those who prefer their God to be personified. There is much confusion in the west over the apparent polytheism of Hinduism. Gods abound: Vishnu, Shiva, Kali, Brahma, Ganesha, Hanuman, Rama, Krishna, etc. But there is really only one God/ground of being in Hinduism: *Brahman*. Hinduism is a monist system, particularly in the Advaita Vedanta tradition that I draw from in this book. Advaita means "non-dual" – dvaita is "dual" – so this spiritual system is by definition monistic, non-dual. The Gods and *devas* we encounter in the colorful system of Hinduism are mythical personifications of various aspects of Brahman, the true reality. This habitual personification honors the need in many of us to worship, or at least revere, a more human-like form than the highly abstract nonduality that is Brahman.

Many of the Advaita Vedanta temples in the United States today were built as part of the Ramakrishna school of Advaita Vedanta. Ramakrishna was a 19th Century saint and mystic who is said to have existed almost perpetually in *Samadhi/gnosis.* Vivekananda was his most influential proselytizer and it is Vivekananda's work that led to the success of the Ramakrishna school in the West. In Ramakrishna's temples today there is generally an image of Ramakrishna himself. This image exists to aid those who are inclined to revere or worship personifications of holiness. We need not believe that Ramakrishna was a divine figure, different in kind from mere mortals such as ourselves, to revere him. Indeed, his existence was not different in kind from ours. He merely had the good fortune to live in God-realization more than most of us will ever enjoy. It's all a matter of degree. For this reason he may be revered. But we can revere literally any person or anything if it helps us transcend our little self and realize our true Self. Christ is the most common personification of God in the West. Unfortunately, his message, as has been discussed, is often obscured in the mainline traditions. If we see past the power politics to his underlying message of *gnosis* he becomes a highly effective object of reverence or worship in the *bhakti yoga* tradition.

These yogas do not, of course, exhaust the paths to God. In the system I advocate, the complete spirituality of Self-realization may be arrived at either through sudden insight, through decades of meditation, through decades of devotion, through decades of work, or through sheer luck. Life itself is praxis, every waking and dreaming moment of it. Any activity can be a praxis. Tennis can be a praxis and there is in fact a wonderful book on *The Inner Game of Tennis* that stresses Buddhist teachings in the difficult game of tennis that may be extended to all life situations. Relationships with loved ones, with neighbors, even with "enemies," are also praxis. We learn from each interaction and we can implement what we have learned to try and live as our true Self.

But the surest means to Self-realization is to find an established path that resonates with you and your intuitions and follow it to its end. Ultimately, the path we choose matters less than finding a path and sticking with it. Each path is unique and no one can tell us what is our best path. Spiritual democracy is thus assured.

Chapter 31: Turn darkness into light by becoming Christ-like, Buddha-like

Many who encounter Buddha's teachings find themselves challenged immediately by Buddha's starting point: that all life is suffering. Buddha's Four Noble Truths start with this assertion, and continue by asserting that the root of suffering is desire or grasping, that there is a way to end this grasping and that this way is the Eightfold Path. The Sanskrit word that is normally translated as "suffering," *dukkha*, is, however, better translated as "frustration." Buddha's teaching was not, then, that all life is necessarily suffering, but rather that all of normal life inevitably leads to frustration. (What follows is not a view of Buddhism that all Buddhists would share. It is, however, in my view, most in keeping with Buddha's original insights).

The legend of Buddha's origin has him growing up in a royal family surrounded by outrageous privilege. Due to a prophecy upon his birth that he would become either a great spiritual or a great political leader, his parents, members of the ruling *kshatriya* caste in India, insulated him from normal human life. He was confined to the palace and its grounds and was not allowed to see signs of normal human suffering, in an ill-conceived effort to force the young Siddhartha (the Buddha's human name) into the political path. Siddhartha escaped the palace, as we would expect, at some point in his early adult life, and encountered the unpleasantness of sickness, old age and death. These encounters awakened in him a great desire to learn more about the less pleasant aspects of life than had been his lot in the palace. He traveled widely, seeking and finding the great mystics and philosophers of his time. He eventually pursued the ascetic path to spirituality, becoming so thin from fasting that his spine could be seen from the front. He abandoned this path after realizing it was just another kind of extremism that did not ultimately lead to awakening. His final awakening, in which he became the fully enlightened Buddha who started a major world religion/philosophy, occurred when he realized his true Self. As he sat under the bodhi tree, pushing through the last remaining veils of *maya*, illusion, he became the universe, he became God. He devoted the rest of his long life to helping others to wake up, to realize who they are.

So what did Buddha mean by his noble truth that all life is frustration? Wasn't his own achievement of awakening good evidence that all of life is not frustration? In a word, yes. Like most simplifications, the full teaching is often lost if we focus merely on the phrase "life is suffering" or "life is frustration." The deeper meaning behind this teaching is that even though there are undeniably pleasant experiences in life, such as finding love, achieving career goals, having a family, winning admiration and respect of friends, among others, all of these happy occasions inevitably lead to some degree of frustration. This is the case because love too often fades or leads to heartbreak;

career success can be fleeting, family members can desert us or will eventually die, and the admiration of friends can be especially fleeting. And eventually we all die, the final frustration. More generally, all "good" things pre-suppose that we know what is "bad." The root of frustration is the constant grasping innate to human life. By eliminating, or, more realistically, reducing grasping, we can eventually wake up to our true Self. And as mentioned in previous chapters, by awakening to our true Self the final frustration of death is seen to be mostly illusory. The true Self continues for eternity.

But isn't seeking to know our true Self a kind of grasping? Yes, and this is where the over-simplification of a phrase is again misleading. Picking up a book to read about Buddha is a kind of grasping, a kind of desire. Doing *anything* at all, literally, entails grasping. Getting out of bed is grasping. Breathing is grasping. Eating is grasping. It's all grasping. We cannot be alive and not grasp. The trick is to grasp, insofar as is possible, only those things that lead to improved knowledge of our true Self. But that's just the first part of the trick. The second part is to grasp only as tight as is necessary to achieve the knowledge of Self. We dance through life with grace. Grace is the soft grasping that Buddha advocated. Grace is movement, action, without jarring ourselves or others. Grace requires that we honor the present moment, secure in our knowledge of our true Self.

This is how we turn darkness into light. Events happen in all of our lives that we can't help interpreting, at first, as bad. This tendency is in-built and not easily overcome. These "bad" events can be as insignificant as a stranger who declines to return your smile, a rude comment from a friend, or a thoughtless driver cutting you off. More seriously, perhaps we are fired unjustly from a job we enjoy, we suffer financial hardship and lose our home, we are left by someone we love, or we suffer from injury or disease. Too often, we let such events affect us negatively and many of us lash out at others, passing on these unhealthy moments to others as an expression of our own frustrations.

We can, however, through the praxis of everyday life, turn such dark moments into light. Rather than perpetuating the cycle of unhealthy emotions, we can, with knowledge of Self and with our knowledge that all life is lived only in the present moment, choose to interpret the events around us as mere experience, as blessed experience. It's all just experience. We should suspend judgment and choose instead to enjoy it. Even the bad stuff. We approach all experience with grace and we thus inspire grace in others.

Some events seem so bad that it is impossible to turn them into light. The death of a loved one is such a moment. We cannot, as embodied humans, take such an event with pure equanimity. At least not at first. It takes time to see such events from the true Self's point of view. Again, we must find that balance between knowing our true Self and living as human beings, with eons of biological history behind us. Eventually, however, we can approach even such extreme events as the death of a loved one from the higher view of the Self.

Through this trained ability, this *praxis*, we become Christ-like, we become Buddha-like.

As we grow our world, so we grow ourselves

Christopher Hunt, 20th Century British-American
philosopher
(and the author's father)

Chapter 32: Emotional punctuation is unavoidable and not entirely fruitless

Isn't all of this hopelessly high-minded and impractical? Can we really live our lives like this? Should we?

Alan Watts writes that a Zen master is, at the end of the day, just a human being. And mountains are just mountains. Zen also teaches that a Zen master doesn't necessarily peel potatoes for dinner any differently than an unenlightened person. The Zen master realizes, rather, that peeling potatoes *is* Zen practice. He laughs at jokes like all of us, he gets frustrated at life's vagaries, and he displays the full range of human emotions. This range of human emotions is what I mean by "emotional punctuation." Just as sleeping or eating punctuate our days, so emotions punctuate our experience. And this isn't entirely fruitless or unhealthy.

It seems that the best way to balance the lofty spiritual principles I've described here with the practicality of everyday life and our own biology is to metaphorically step back a little bit. There is a risk in pursuing spiritual awakening overzealously. We can "stink of Zen," as Watts describes, if we get a bit too into it. It can in fact become unhealthy if we, in the process of seeking spiritual truth, ignore aspects of our little selves that won't let themselves be ignored. And we are all, of course, quite different from each other. For example, if we are trying to avoid expressing anger while playing tennis, because it's an unhelpful emotion in the game, it can result in more anger and frustration. This can happen if, despite our efforts to let anger and frustration go, we still become angry at missing an easy shot. We may then become angry at ourselves for expressing this frustration... This is obviously not productive.

The solution is to step back a little from our behavior and even our thoughts (whether this is really possible or not, let's use it as a metaphor) and simply observe. Observe the frustration, its causes and how it manifested. And gently seek to reduce our frustration in similar situations in the future. We should never become frustrated with ourselves for expressing frustration! Simply step back, observe, and work diligently, through whatever praxis we prefer, to improve our responses in the future.

Through this practice we can eventually achieve a generally more calm state of mind and a choice in each moment in how we react to the world around us. We can choose to act with less fear, less anger, less knee-jerk resentment, when we recognize that these may be our default emotions to many of life's more difficult situations. And we can also choose to let love infuse our being when our more default reaction would be to let anger or fear take over.

The bottomline is that we, as human beings, will never rid ourselves entirely of emotional punctuation – the normal ups and downs of life. And nor should we want to entirely rid ourselves of this punctuation. Without emotion of any kind, there is no life. Life is, at its root, emotion. Luckily (or not) the primary emotion throughout the entire universe is love. The solution that practical mysticism leads us to is balance. We should strive toward a balance between our normal human emotions and the behavior inspired by knowledge of our true Self. This is a process with no specific endpoint.

God is love.

John, 4:16

Chapter 33: We are suspended in an ocean of pure love

God is love, and we are it. This is all the spirituality we need. In closing this book, I return to this theme because it is the good news that should be proclaimed from every news outlet every day. Our alarm clocks should wake us with a repeated mantra of "God is love, and you are it." Comforted with such knowledge, we would experience a mini-*gnosis* with every waking moment. The combined effect may lead to the more complete *gnosis* that has been the source of every spiritual movement since the dawn of time.

We are indeed suspended in an ocean of pure love. If Brahman/God constitutes the totality of existence, and Brahman/God is pure love, everything around us is pure love. And if we are it, we are pure love. The Self is pure love.

We can go further, however. Even if we focus on our little selves, we see that our little selves are suspended in this same ocean. Merely by being, we exist in love. *To be* means we are connected to the rest of the universe, and to the deeper reality of Brahman. This ocean of inter-connections consists of information, causality, energy, matter, mind – all words for the same thing – which is ultimately just love.

We can, as embodied human beings, with many billions of years of earthly and cosmic evolution behind us – and many more billions of years in front of us – know these truths and live these truths. We can find the balance between our various little fragmented selves and our true Self. The entirety of life is our true *praxis* and we advance that practice with each breath taken through the realization that we only live in the present moment. Each breath is the inspiration and expiration of pure love. All is love. Love is All. And we are it.